When Things Just Don't Make Sense

When Things Just Don't Make Sense

Navigating the Unexplainables of Life
from the Christian Perspective

by
Frank R. Shivers

Unless otherwise noted, Scripture quotations are from
The Holy Bible *King James Version*

Library of Congress Cataloging-in-Publication Data

Shivers, Frank R., 1949-
When Things Just Don't Make Sense / Frank Shivers
ISBN 978-1-878127-47-1

Library of Congress Control Number:
2021920994

Cover design by
Tim King

For Information:
Frank Shivers Evangelistic Association
P. O. Box 9991
Columbia, South Carolina 29290
www.frankshivers.com

"I would sooner walk in the dark and hold hard to a promise of God than to trust in the light of the brightest day that ever dawned."[1]
~ C. H. Spurgeon

Publications by Frank R. Shivers

"We are not writing upon water but carving upon imperishable material."[2] ~ C. H. Spurgeon

The Treasure of Grace
Persecuted for Christ's Sake
When Things Just Don't Make Sense
When the Rain Comes
Christian Basics 101
Grief Beyond Measure, but Not Beyond Grace
Grief Beyond Measure, but Not Beyond Grace (Funeral Home Version)
Growing Old, Honorably and Happily
The Wounded Spirit
The Wounded Spirit: Companion Workbook
Growing in Knowledge, Living by Faith
Marriage and Parenting Boosters
Caught Up to Heaven
Expositions of the Psalms (Three Volumes)
Life Principles from Proverbs
The Evangelism Apologetic Study Bible
Hot Buttons on Apologetics
Hot Buttons on Morality
Hot Buttons on Discipleship
The Pornography Trap
The Poison of Porn
Heavy Stuff
Heavy Stuff (Student Workbook)
Clear Talk to Students
Nuggets of Truth (Three Volumes)
Soulwinning 101
Spurs to Soulwinning
Evangelistic Preaching 101
Evangelistic Praying
The Evangelistic Invitation 101

The Minister and the Funeral
Revivals 101
Children Sermons That Connect
Be Careful Little Eyes
How to Preach Without Evangelistic Results (Pamphlet)
False Hopes of Heaven (Tract)
First Steps for New Believers (Tract)
The Goal Line Stand (Tract)
The Death Clock (Tract)

PRESENTED TO

_____

BY

_____

DATE

_____

"If you ask, 'Why is this happening?' no light may come; but if you ask, 'How am I to glorify God now?' there will always be an answer."[3]

~ J. I. Packer

To

James Hartman

The investment of time and labor Jim has expended freely in helping the Frank Shivers Evangelistic Association and me personally over the past 40 years is incalculable. His expertise as a financial advisor, insurance agent, and retirement planner is unsurpassable and has benefited both my ministry and me immensely. His friendship, encouragement, and support for the work I do as an evangelist are invaluable.

"Every crisis has the potential to empower and purify us, to make us more valuable servants in His kingdom. God does not waste our sorrows."[4]

~ David Jeremiah

Contents

Whate'er my God ordains is right;
　　　His holy will abideth.
I will be still, whate'er He doth,
　　　And follow where He guideth.
He is my God; though dark my road,
He holds me that I shall not fall,
Wherefore to Him I leave it all.

Whate'er my God ordains is right;
　　　He never will deceive me.
He leads me by the proper path;
　　　I know He will not leave me.
I take, content, what He hath sent;
His hand can turn my griefs away,
And patiently I wait His day.

Whate'er my God ordains is right;
　　　Though now this cup, in drinking,
May bitter seem to my faint heart,
　　　I take it, all unshrinking.
My God is true; each morn anew
Sweet comfort yet shall fill my heart,
And pain and sorrow shall depart.

Whate'er my God ordains is right;
　　　Here shall my stand be taken.
Though sorrow, need, or death be mine,
　　　Yet am I not forsaken.
My Father's care is round me there;
He holds me that I shall not fall,
And so to Him I leave it all.

　　　　　　　　~ Samuel Rodigast (1675)

Introduction

Some things that happen are hard to understand, and they test the strongest believer's faith. C. H. Spurgeon states, "God's designs are vast and far-reaching, and His methods are frequently strange and inscrutable, though always wise."[5] Jerry Bridges states, "The sovereignty of God is often questioned because man does not understand what God is doing. Because He does not act as we think He should, we conclude He cannot act as we think He would."[6]

James Dobson writes, "Unfortunately, many young believers—and some older ones, too—do not know that there will be times in every person's life when circumstances don't add up, when God doesn't appear to make sense. This aspect of the Christian faith is not well advertised."[7] Chuck Swindoll agrees, saying, "God's heavenly plan doesn't always make earthly sense."[8] Even the Apostle Paul said, "O the depth of the riches both of the wisdom and knowledge of God! how unsearchable [undiscoverable; unfathomable) are His judgments, and his ways past finding out [untraceable]!" (Romans 11:33). R. E. Murphy said, "God's secret, or unsearchability, is proof of divine power—these are secrets that humans cannot even guess. What God does not reveal demonstrates who God really is."[9]

Barna Research Group made the inquiry: "If you could ask God one question and you knew He would give you an answer, what would you ask?" The most common response was, "Why is there pain and suffering in the world?" The strongest of saints have episodes in life when what God allows to happen doesn't make sense, such as the severe pain and suffering of a godly man; the manner of death of a family member or friend; the untimely death of an effective evangelical preacher; the human atrocities that inflict harm and death; a crippling accident, dementia, or serious disease; the allowing of a socialistic, anti-Christian political platform to rule a nation; or a viral disease that kills millions and hinders the advance of global missions. Some things just don't make sense.

It didn't make sense to Mary and Martha that Jesus delayed His coming to heal their brother Lazarus (John 11:21). It didn't make sense to Job why he experienced such devastating loss and physical suffering (he wasn't privy to the conversation Satan and God had regarding his testing, Job 1:6–12). It didn't make sense to Abraham why God told him to slay his son Isaac on Mount Carmel (Genesis 22:2). It didn't make sense to Sarah that she would give birth to a child at the age of 90 (Genesis 17:19). It didn't make sense to Joseph that God would allow him to be falsely accused by Potiphar's wife and imprisoned innocently (Genesis 39:7–20). Kirk Johnson, a friend whose critical bout with COVID-19 didn't make sense, prompted the writing and title of this book. Likewise, perhaps, something has transpired or is happening in your life that just doesn't correlate with your religious belief, convictions or understanding about God—something that just doesn't make sense—and it's thrown your world, and perhaps faith, into chaos.

It doesn't always make sense:

When the fig tree doesn't bud
When there are no grapes on the vine
When the olive crop fails
When the fields produce no food
When there are no sheep in the pen
When there are no cattle in the stalls
~ Habakkuk 3:17

What do we do when what happens just don't make sense? We trust and rely upon God. We pray for His coping strength and grace so that we may endure. And we exhibit unwavering faith in the goodness, justice, love, and fairness of God. Elton Trueblood said, "Faith is not belief without proof, but trust without reservation."[10] We choose to do as Habakkuk: "Yet I will [choose to] rejoice in the Lord; I will [choose to] shout in exultation in the [victorious] God of my salvation!" (Habakkuk 3:18 AMP). What we don't do is panic, worry and fear, or become bitter and angry with God or discouraged beyond hope in the despair. Despite what happens or how it happens, Jesus said, "Let not your heart be troubled" (John 14:1). Spurgeon said, "There are many sorts of broken hearts, and Christ is good at healing them all."[11] Greg Laurie states, "We don't determine what challenges, what hardships, or what difficulties come our way. All we determine is how we will react to those things when they come."[12] It's prudent that all new believers understand up front, lest their faith be dashed, that Christians are not exempt from being crushed with a seemingly bad, senseless happening that comes unexpectedly and without explanation. This book certainly would be a resource to help in that regard.

> Under the shadow of Your throne,
> Your saints have dwelt secure;
> Sufficient is Your arm alone,
> And our defense is sure.
> ~ Isaac Watts (1719)

Man's abiding comfort and security in a changing (and dying) body and time of bizarre happenings is in the eternal stability, dependability, immutability, and trustworthiness of God (Psalm 90:2). And that is the foundational undergirding of all that is stated herewith.

> When nothing whereon to lean remains,
> When strongholds crumble to dust,
> When nothing is sure but that God still reigns,
> That is just the time to trust.[13]
> ~ Unknown

"What a wonderful God we have—He is the Father of our Lord Jesus Christ, the source of every mercy, and the One who so wonderfully comforts and strengthens us in our hardships and trials. And why does He do this? So that when others are troubled, needing our sympathy and encouragement, we can pass on to them this same help and comfort God has given us. You can be sure that the more we undergo sufferings for Christ, the more He

will shower us with His comfort and encouragement"
(2 Corinthians 1:3–5 TLB).

1   Don't Trust Human Reasoning

"God loves to be consulted. Therefore, take all thy difficulties to be resolved by Him. Be in the habit of going to Him in the first place—before self-wisdom, human friends."[14] ~ Charles Bridges

What do we do when something happens that just doesn't make sense? Paul said, "At present we are men looking at *puzzling reflections* in a mirror. The time will come when we shall see reality whole and face to face! At present all I know is a little fraction of the truth, but the time will come when I shall know it as fully as God now knows me!" (1 Corinthians 13:12 PHILLIPS). So, what do we do amidst puzzling and seemingly senseless circumstances? We trust God, not human reasoning. We are to look outside of self to God for understanding, wisdom and guidance. We are to live by faith in God, not faith in worldly rationale or humanistic philosophy. "Human insights are never enough. God's ways are incomprehensible (Romans 11:33–34); yet He is trustworthy."[15] "When the believer is in Christ, faith points the way to higher circles of truth."[16]

Octavius Winslow states, "How constantly is the human mind tempted to speculate and philosophize and reason about Divine truth [or happenings]—to attempt to sound that which is unfathomable; to unveil that for which there is no clue; to understand that which baffles speculation, transcends reason, and, like Him whose truth it is, enfolds itself in inexplicable and awful mystery! Let reason give way to faith; and pride to humility; and vain speculation to adoring wonder, gratitude, and love."[17]

What counsel doth Solomon (the wisest man that ever lived) give about the unexplainables of life? He says, "Trust in the LORD with all thine heart; and lean not unto thine own understanding" (Proverbs 3:5). "Trust" ("entire reliance upon Jehovah"[18]) in the LORD with "all" (totality; an undivided heart) thine "heart" (with the entire mind); and "lean" ("signifies 'to lean upon, rest upon,' just as man rests upon a spear for support"[19]) not unto thine own "understanding"

("It is on God, not on thyself, that thou art commanded to depend. He who trusts in his own heart is a fool"[20]; don't rely upon personal insights, discernment or impressions, impulsiveness). The believer's sure refuge in the inexplicable and bad times is found in only one place—absolute trustfulness in God's just and holy character and goodness to His children.

Charles Simeon said, "But who receives everything as from God? Who looks to him to order everything in his behalf! Who realizes the idea that not a sparrow falls to the ground without the special appointment of God? Who has not his attention so fixed on second causes, as almost to overlook the First great Cause of all? It is undeniable that men are universally 'leaning to their own understanding,' or 'saying to the fine gold, thou art my confidence.'"[21] The anchor to our ship in the time of confounding and baffling storms is absolute trust in and reliance (dependence) upon God and His promises (Proverbs 22:19).

Matthew Henry summarizes, "We must believe that God is able to do what He will; wise to do what is best; and good, according to His promise, to do what is best for us, if we love Him, and serve Him. We must, with an entire submission and satisfaction, depend upon Him to perform all things for us and not lean to our own understanding. In all our conduct we must be diffident [distrustful, doubtful] of our own judgment and confident of God's wisdom, power, and goodness."[22] "All he asks," says Chuck Swindoll, "is that we trust Him, that we stand before Him in integrity and faith. God is just waiting for us to trust Him."[23]

2   When God's Footsteps Are Unknown

"Thy way is in the sea, and thy path in the great waters, and thy footsteps are not known." ~ Psalm 77:19

What do we do when something happens that just doesn't make sense, when God's "footsteps" are unknown in it all? We respond like Martin Luther, who pleaded to know God 's mind about a matter that occurred. He said, it seemed, as if he heard God speak to him, saying, "I am not to be traced."[24] That echoes the experience of many saints. With Luther, we have learned that God does much for which He gives no accounting (His "footsteps are not known"). Samuel Slater says, "He often goeth so much out of our sight that we are unable to give an account of what He doeth or what He is about to do."[25] "Although the works of God," states John Calvin, "are in part manifest to us, yet all our knowledge of them comes far short of their immeasurable height. [They] far surpass the limited powers of our understanding."[26] God's footsteps "in the sea" of man's adversities are inscrutable. "God's way is incomprehensible, though undoubtedly right; in His holiness lies the answer to the enigmas [conundrums, puzzlements]."[27]

'His way is in the sea and His path in the great waters, and His footsteps are not known' (Psalm 77:19). Spurgeon says, "None can follow Thy tracks by foot or eye. Thou art alone in Thy glory, and Thy ways are hidden from mortal ken. Thy purposes Thou wilt accomplish, but the means are often concealed; indeed, they are in themselves too vast and mysterious for human understanding."[28] The actions of God defy human comprehension and will remain in part a mystery until He chooses to interpret them. That which is known is that God promises to take the sorrows of life (the unexplainables, senseless, unfair) and supernaturally use them for good in the lives of His children and to benefit His kingdom on earth (Romans 8:28). Jerry Bridges says, "Confidence in the sovereignty of God in all that affects us is crucial to our trusting Him."[29]

Let us trust God, when we cannot trace Him. "There are times when it must be enough for us simply to know that He is acting, and that on our behalf and for our good. At such seasons we must pre-eminently 'walk by faith, and not by sight.' He chooses that the method of His dealings should be hidden, and we have no right to urge Him to withdraw the veil. And how often has there been a footstep of God where we have not discerned it! We had an illness or a bereavement or a disappointment or a loss; the world said, "How unfortunate!" But God passed our way; the world could not see His footprint—blessed were we if we could."[30]

3 The Unexplainable Why

"We may be frankly bewildered at things that happen to us, but God knows exactly what he is doing, and what he is after, in his handling of our affairs. Always, and in everything, he is wise: we shall see that hereafter, even where we never saw it here."[31] ~ J. I. Packer

What do we do when something happens that just doesn't make sense? Asking the why of an illness, terminal disease, crippling or deadly accident, or unexpected death is natural. The ultimate, complete, and satisfying answer to the question, however, is unknown. What is known is that its primary cause springs from the fallen world in which we live. Sickness, suffering, sorrow, and death were unknown in the Garden of Eden prior to man's fall into sin. Vance Havner said, "You need never ask why, because Calvary covers it all. When before the throne we stand in Him complete, all the riddles that puzzle us here will fall into place, and we shall know in fulfillment what we now believe in faith—that all things work together for good in His eternal purpose. No longer will we cry, 'My God, why?' 'Alas' will become 'Alleluia,' all question marks will be straightened into exclamation points, sorrow will change to singing, and pain will be lost in praise."[32]

Across some of our days, God marks, "Will explain later."[33] Until then, we trust His heart and live by His promise that "all things work together for good to them that love God, to them who are the called according to his purpose" (Romans 8:28). Presently, the "good" that will evolve from your sickness, suffering, or sorrow may not be known. But Jesus is still saying, "What I do thou knowest not now; but thou shalt know [if not now, then] hereafter" (John 13:7). Upon that you may confidently depend.

"So sublime is Providence," writes Spurgeon, "that we do not comprehend it; so good is it that we are filled with wonder as we see its designs unfolded. We see its bright side at times and sun ourselves in the warm light thereof, and then we adore and magnify the Lord. At other times we have felt the night side of providence and have sorrowed in its chill shade; yea, and perhaps we have even rebelled against it; and yet at that very time the Lord's purposes have been divinely rich toward us, and the night has been the choicest season of benediction. We have not the wings of eagles on which to soar to the exceeding height of the dealings of the Lord; we walk below and look up wonderingly, as men gaze on the stars: we are sure that we are safe beneath the sublime all-covering power, but we are equally clear that the longest experience and the profoundest thought will never measure the height of the thoughts and ways of the Eternal."[34] See Isaiah 55:8–9.

4   God Is in Control of What Happens

"God is not a bewildered bellhop running up and down the corridors of the hotel He created trying to find the right key."[35]
~ R. G. Lee

What do we do when something happens that just doesn't make sense? We acknowledge that God orders the steps of the righteous man (Psalm 37:23) from the rising of the sun to the going down of the same and all the night through to the time of his death (the child of God "cannot be torn from this earth one hour ahead of the time which God has appointed, and he cannot be detained on earth one moment after God is done with him here."[36]) With David we say in confident hope, "But I trust in you, O Lord; I say, 'You are my God.' My times ['The various vicissitudes of my life'[37]] are in your hand" (Psalm 31:14-15 ESV). "'My times are in Thy hand'—the seasons, the stages and eras of my life, with all their casualties and opportunities, incidents and events, are all in Thy hand, under Thy control and at Thy disposal."[38] David sings, "'The course of my life is in Your power.' This to him was a most cheering fact; he had no fear as to his circumstances since all things were in the divine hands."[39] W. S. Plummer says, "The whole of life, with all that threatens it, with all that continues it, is in the hand of the wise, good, powerful, perfect ruler of all things."[40]

Adrian Rogers reminds the saint, "Nothing can touch the life of a child of God unless God ordains or allows it. Everything is Father-filtered through the loving hand and sovereign will of God. Therefore, even in trials and tribulations, we can rest in Him!"[41] The believer is never in the grip of blind forces.[42] See Psalm 121:8. Such an understanding led Henry Martyn to say, "I am immortal until God's work for me to do is done."[43] Knowing that our times are under His divine superintendency instills comfort, confidence and calm in the face of that which happens that doesn't make earthly sense. It allays fears and anxieties about our family, friends loved greater than ourselves, and personal suffering and pain (Psalm 37:23).

Andrew Murray explains: "In times of trouble, the trusting child of God may say, 'First, He brought me here. It is by His will that I'm in this great place. Next, He will keep me here in His love and give me grace in this trial to behave as His child. Then He will make the trial a blessing, teaching me the lessons He intends for me to learn and working in the grace He means to bestow. And in His good time, He can bring me out again. How and when—He knows.'"[44]

My times are in Your hand;
My God, I wish them there!
My life, my friends, my soul I leave
Entirely to Your care.
                    ~ W. F. Lloyd (1824)

"The Oriental shepherd," states F. B. Meyer, "was always ahead of his sheep. He was in front. Any attempt upon them had to take him into account. Now God is down in front. He is in the tomorrows. It is tomorrow that fills men with dread. But God is there already, and all tomorrows of our life have to pass before Him before they can get to us."[45]

5   Stop Trying to Figure God Out

"It's not about figuring out all of the mysteries of God, but embracing Him and cherishing Him—even when He doesn't make perfect sense to us."[46] ~ Francis Chan

What do we do when something happens that just doesn't make sense? We stop trying to figure God and His ways out and simply trust Him with the unknown. Why? 'His judgments and His ways are past finding out' (Romans 11:33). "Past finding out" means "that which cannot be traced out" or "that which cannot be tracked out."[47] "The word could be used of a bloodhound who found it impossible to follow the scent of a criminal, or of a guide who could not trace out or follow a poorly marked path in the woods."[48] There are some things that God does that are not within man's ability to rationally resolve. Our finite brains are just too small, too inferior. Other things are divine secrets not to be sought out (Deuteronomy 29:29). James Dobson writes, "When you think about it, there is comfort in the approach to life's trials and tribulations. We are relieved from the responsibility of trying to figure them out. We haven't been given enough information to decipher the code. It is enough to acknowledge that God makes sense even when He doesn't make sense."[49]

William MacDonald states, "His decisions are unsearchable; they are too deep for mortal minds to fully understand. The ways in which He arranges creation, history, redemption, and providence are beyond our limited comprehension."[50] Matthew Henry remarked, "We know not what He designs. When the wheels are set in motion and Providence has begun to work, yet we know not what he has in view; it is past finding out."[51] Spurgeon comments, "Our thoughts must forever be weak and fragmentary as compared with His thoughts. God's designs are vast and far-reaching, and His methods are frequently strange and inscrutable, though always wise. Oftentimes He brings light of excessive brightness out of darkness more dense than usual, and produces superior joys out of extraordinary sorrows."[52] See Isaiah 55:8–9; Job 5:9 and Job 26:14.

No man can put God in a box and figure out the rhyme and reason of His actions. Its futile to try.

Man can only trust Him with that which happens for his best good (Romans 8:28). Wholeheartedly surrender to God, leaving quietly with Him all the "whys" and "what ifs" and "but what abouts."

6   Learn to Kiss the Wave

"Trials come to prove and improve us."[53] ~ Augustine

What do we do when something happens that just doesn't make sense? We must change the question from, "Why did this happen *to* me?" to "Why did this happen *for* me?" (benefit, purpose). That one-word change brings a huge *shift* not only to the question but to its answer. Spurgeon undoubtedly made that word change, for he kissed the waves of affliction, counting them as a blessing. He purportedly said, "I have learned to kiss the wave that throws me against the Rock of Ages."[54] The waves of affliction (some I'm sure he thought unjust and unfair) that billowed upon Spurgeon often in his life forced him to cling to Christ, the Rock of Ages, for healing, help, and hope. He, therefore, "kissed" the wave (counted it blessed), for it was a means of increasing His dependency upon Christ, and the deepening of his faith. Spurgeon said, "I am certain that I never did grow in grace one-half so much anywhere as I have upon the bed of pain."[55] We, too, can learn to "kiss the wave" of affliction (graciously bear it) when its "side effects" (benefit, gain) of maturing faith, divine insight, and the development of greater dependency and trust upon God are firmly realized.

The same "waves" that bring seasickness (pain, distress, being distraught, confusion) bring peace, consolation and dependency upon God when allowed to force us to cling to the Rock of Ages. Instead of cursing the waves, may we "kiss" them for the good they accomplish in the inner recesses of our soul. The psalmist said, "It was good for me to suffer, so that I might learn your statutes" (Psalm 119:71 NET). Don't bash the "waves" of suffering. Embrace them as part of His mysterious plan to make you more like Him (Romans 12:1–2 and Romans 8:28). "Blessed be any wind that blows us into the port of our Savior's love!"[56]

I will kiss the battering waves that assail,
Knowing with Christ I shall prevail.
With each wave that batters upon my heart,
Peace, strength and comfort shall He impart.
He my pilot and protector shall be,
Until this part of His plan is finished for me.
~ Frank Shivers (2021)

"The prodigal was never safer than when he was driven to his father's bosom, because he could find sustenance nowhere else. Our Lord favors us with a famine in the land that it may make us seek after Himself the more."[57]

7   No Surprises to God

"God is already prepared for everything you're going to face tomorrow, next week, and next month. What the future holds may surprise us, but it doesn't surprise God. Nothing ever catches Him by surprise or makes Him say, 'Oh, really?'"[58] ~ Rick Warren

What do we do when something happens that just doesn't make sense? We trust in the fact that with God there are no accidents or surprises. He is never blindsided by what happens to His children. The Bible says of God, "Your eyes saw my unformed body; all the days ordained for me were written in your book before one of them came to be" (Psalm 139:16 NIV).

Spurgeon explains, "An architect draws his plans and makes out his specifications; even so did the great Maker of our frame write down all our members in the book of His purposes. God saw us when we could not be seen, and He wrote about us when there was nothing of us to write about, when as yet there were none of our members in existence."[59] Isaiah declares that God knows "the end from the beginning" (Isaiah 46:9–10).

The psalmist said, "You know when I sit down and when I rise up [my entire life, everything I do]; You understand my thought from afar" (Psalm 139:2 AMP). Absolutely nothing that happens to us catches God by surprise. He not only sees what our lot in the future will be, but He also prepares us for it. Surprises (terminal medical diagnosis, severe illness, injury or death to a loved one) can bring horrendous pain and bear enormous impact on our life and that of others. But to know that they come as no surprise to God brings consolation and peace.

> God is not the least surprised or taken off guard by the storms you are facing. Trust Him; He's got this!

"God is not the least surprised or taken off guard by the storms you are facing. Trust Him; He's got this!"[60] David Jeremiah said, "Dealing with life's surprises is a perfect opportunity to understand more about God (that He is never surprised) and see how His attributes [love, holiness, kindness, power, sovereignty, etc.] can help us respond to the surprises we encounter in life."[61]

8   Past Deliverances

"In trouble we are prone to forget all that we have heard and read that makes for our comfort."[62] ~ Richard Sibbes

What do we do when something happens that just doesn't make sense? We continue to trust God's hand of deliverance, as in the past. "Make diligent search into, and call to remembrance what formerly hath been between God and you. The remembrance of former things doth often uphold, when present sense fails."[63] Experience is a good teacher which has taught us to confidently say, "The LORD is my rock, and my fortress, and my deliverer; my God, my strength, in whom I will trust; my buckler, and the horn of my salvation, and my high tower" (Psalm 18:2). See 2 Samuel 22:2 and Psalm 20:7. "It was not the stamp of our foot," says E. J. Robinson, "that quieted the earthquake, not the sound of our voice that stilled the tempest, not the might of our arm that slew the lion, not the power of our hand that rent the network. It was not any creature except as sent by God, armed with a portion of His strength, and for the sake of Jesus Christ, that in any degree accomplished our deliverance."[64]

Joseph Parker said, "Wondrous is one little line in the history: 'And thy rod, wherewith thou smotest the river, take in thine hand, and go,' and afterward Moses, having spoken to Joshua, said, 'I will stand on the top of the hill with the rod of God in mine hand.' Never forget the old rod, the old Book, the old truth—the sword that cut off the head of Goliath. 'Give me that,' said David; 'there is none like it.' Thus, God hides inspiration in things of apparently little value, and touches the imagination and the faith by books, ministries, churches, altars, which we thought had passed away into desuetude, perhaps oblivion. Your first prayer may help you today. The faith of your youth may be the only thing to win the battle which now challenges your strength. One little hour with the old, old Book may be all you need to obtain the sufficiency of light which will drive away the cloud of mystery and bring in the heaven of explanation."[65]

Commemorate and celebrate God's faithfulness on a daily basis, and It will infuse the heart with consolation, peace and hope in every trial that arises. Our God can do again what He did before (Hebrews 13:8).

Be still, my soul; your God will undertake
    To guide the future as He has the past.
Your hope, your confidence let nothing shake;
    All now mysterious shall be bright at last.
Be still, my soul; the waves and winds still know
His voice who ruled them while He dwelt below.
       ~ Katharina von Schlegel (1855)

9 Trust God to Bring Good Out of the Bad

"In the chemistry of the cross, God takes things that in and of themselves are bad, and He puts them together, much as a chemist might take chemicals that in and of themselves may be deleterious and mixes them to make a medicine that brings healing."[66] ~ Adrian Rogers

What do we do when something happens that just doesn't make sense? We trust God to bring good out of the bad that has happened (even when we have no idea how He can). Our heart clings to Romans 8:28 like a grappling hook. The text promises, "And we know that all that happens to us is working for our good if we love God and are fitting into his plans" (Romans 8:28 TLB). Paul doesn't say, "We hope," but, "We know." It's not a conjecture, opinion or wishful thinking; it's a firm declaration of absolute certainty.[67] "No matter what our situation," comments John MacArthur, "our suffering, our persecution, our sinful failure, our pain, our lack of faith—in those things, as well as in all other things, our heavenly Father will work to produce our ultimate victory and blessing."[68] MacArthur continues, "*All things* includes circumstances and events that are good and beneficial in themselves as well as those that are in themselves evil and harmful."[69] All of life's blissful and blastful happenings will mutually cooperate and contribute to our good.[70] Octavius Winslow says "Great trials make great saints. The most deeply afflicted are the most deeply sanctified."[71]

W. A. Criswell states, "Mystery may engulf us, enemies may assail us, friends may desert us, Satan may buffet us, sorrows may overwhelm us, poverty may threaten us, sickness may weaken us, despair may overtake us, dark clouds may swallow us up, but Paul says in this text that all things—those things and a thousand other unnamable things—they all work together for good to them that love God."[72] When life doesn't make sense, trust God to keep His promise to make sense out of the senseless by bringing good from it for our best good. Max Lucado said, "Faith is not the belief that God will do what you want. Faith is the belief that God will do what is right."[73]

10 *When the Unknown Will Be Made Known*

"Evils [that are experienced] *will be so in appearance only and will seem evils only because we cannot read the secret script of God's hidden providence and so cannot discover the ends at which He aims."*[74] ~ A. W. Tozer

What do we do when something happens that just doesn't make sense? We anticipate the day when the fog will be lifted from our eyes and God makes all things clear. In Heaven the senseless happenings of life make sense. Spurgeon says, "We see the providence of God, but it is in a glass, darkly [puzzling, partial clarity, 1 Corinthians 13:12]. We believe all things work together for good to them that love God; we have seen how they work together for good in some cases, and experimentally proved it to be so. But still, it is rather a matter of faith than a matter of sight with us. We cannot tell how 'every dark and bending line meets in the center of His love.' We do not yet perceive how He will make those dark dispensations of trials and afflictions that come upon His people really to subserve His glory and their lasting happiness. But up there we shall see providence, as it were, face to face; and I suppose it will be amongst our greatest surprises, the discovery of how the Lord dealt with us."[75]

J. R. Macduff said, "In this life we have an incomplete view of God's dealings, seeing His plan only half finished and underdeveloped. Yet once we stand in the magnificent temple of eternity, we will have the proper perspective and will see everything fitting gracefully together!"[76] See John 13:7.

Then shall I see and hear and know
All I desired or wished below,
And every power find sweet employ
In that eternal world of joy.
~ Isaac Watts (1719)

11   Trusting God with the Senseless

"Walking by faith means being prepared to trust where we are not permitted to see."[77] ~ John Blanchard

What do we do when something happens that just doesn't make sense? The concise answer is that we hold our ground in trustfulness to God's unfailing faithfulness, compassionate love and caring protection, saying, "Though he slay me, yet will I trust in him" (Job 13:15). We exhibit stubborn, unrelenting, confident faith in God that although we are "in the dark" about the what and why of that which is happening, He isn't. What do we do when something happens that is just off the charts? By faith we say with the psalmist, "Everything GOD does is right—the trademark on all his works is love. GOD'S there, listening for all who pray, for all who pray and mean it. *He does what's best* for those who fear him—hears them call out, and saves them. God *sticks by all who love him*, but it's all over for those who don't" (Psalm 145:17–20 MSG). "We have but to think of the myriads," states Spurgeon, "who have been delivered from all sorts of diseases through the power and virtue of His touch, and we shall joyfully put ourselves in His hands. We trust Him, and sin dies; we love Him, and grace lives; we wait for Him, and grace is strengthened; we see Him as he is, and grace is perfected forever."[78]

Rick Warren said, "The situations that will stretch your faith most will be those times when life falls apart and God is nowhere to be found. This happened to Job."[79] Are you allowing anything to disturb your heart, or allowing any questions to come in which are unsound or dubious? You have to get to the point of the absolute and unquestionable relationship with Christ that takes everything exactly as it comes from Him in perfect trust.[80] "Faith," says F. B. Meyers, "is conscious that God is there."[81] In the time of infirmity, affliction or adversity, faith enables the believer to answer the question addressed to the grieving Shunamite mother, "Is it well with thee?" with her confident answer, "It is well" (2 Kings 4:26).

Whatever my lot, Thou hast taught me to say,
"It is well; it is well with my soul."
~ Horatio Spafford

Alan Redpath said, "There is nothing—no circumstance, no trouble, no testing—that can ever touch me until, first of all, it has gone past God and past Christ right through to me. If it has come that far, it has come with a great purpose, *which I may not understand at the moment.* But as I refuse to become panicky, as I lift up my eyes to Him and accept it as coming from the throne of God for some great purpose of blessing to my own heart, no sorrow will ever disturb me, no trial will ever disarm me, no circumstance will cause me to fret—for I shall rest in the joy of what my Lord is! That is the rest of victory!"[82] John Wesley said, "The bottom of the soul may be in repose even while we are in many outward troubles, just as the bottom of the sea is calm while the surface is strongly agitated."[83]

John Newton said, "Faith upholds a Christian under all trials, by assuring him that every painful dispensation [disbursement, allotment] is under the direction of his Lord; that the season, measure, and continuance of his sufferings are appointed by Infinite Wisdom and designed to work for his everlasting good; and that grace and strength shall be afforded him, according to his need."[84] Job believed that to be true. Even while sitting in the ash pit, Job trusts God enough to say, "What? shall we receive good at the hand of God, and shall we not receive evil? In all this did not Job sin with his lips" (Job 2:10). Abraham faced the unknown by faith, trusting God's promises to sustain (Hebrews 11:8). With Job and him, by faith, place the unknowns, uncertainties and unexplainables of life in the divine hand of God, resting in His promises (Ecclesiastes 9:1 and Psalm 89:13–15). He was proven faithful and true by them, and will be by you as well.

12 Held by God's Hand

"Storms may be howling and blowing, but Jesus is holding my hand."[85] ~ Alfred Barratt

What do we do when something happens that just doesn't make sense? We refuse to fear or panic, because of God's promise to bear us up in the hardest of trial. He says, "Fear thou not; for I am with thee: be not dismayed; for I am thy God: I will strengthen thee; yea, I will help thee; yea, I will uphold thee with the right hand [emblem of omnipotent power] of my righteousness." (Isaiah 41:10).

A young child awaiting severe surgery was asked if he could withstand it. "Yes," was his reply, "if father will hold my hand." In life's trials, feeling the grasp of God's hand incites calm and courage. In the time of the unexplainable, unknowable and painful, we want the omnipotent hand of the omnipresent, omniscient eternal God in our hand. And this the believer is promised. E.L. Hull says, "The grasp of the hand is significant of close and present friendship, of the living nearness of the deliverer. And that sense of God's presence, so near that our faith can touch His hand and hear the deep still music of His voice, realized as it may be in Christ, is the source of a courage which no danger can dispel, no suffering exhaust, and no death destroy."[86] The promise pictures the Lord walking hand in hand with the believer through the sunshine and rain of life. Spurgeon says, "Child of God, see where thou art. Thou art completely in the hand of God. Thou art absolutely and entirely, and in every respect, placed at the will and disposal of Him who is thy God."[87] Our grip on Him may waver, but never will His on us.

There's no other friend on whom I can depend;
Blessed Jesus, hold my hand.
~ Albert E. Brumley

13 Lean into the Strength of God

"The Gospel infuses hope and joy into our current circumstances by acknowledging God's greatness over any crisis we'll face."[88]
~ Randy Alcorn

What do we do when something happens that just doesn't make sense? We lean into the omnipotent strength of God, who says, "I will strengthen thee" (Isaiah 41:10). "God will renew not merely such strength as is natural to us, but a surplusage of strength. In the strength of heavenly food and drink, Elijah 'went forty days and forty nights.'"[89] To him that is downcast, in despair, ready to faint beneath the burden borne, the tender voice of God says, "I will strengthen thee." As Elijah's strength was renewed at the brook Cherith, likewise will be all that are weak who wait upon the Lord (1 Kings 17:4). John Trapp states, "I will [strengthen thee], I will, I will. Oh, the rhetoric of God! Oh! The certainty of the promise."[90]

In the desert grows a plant that derives its name from its very nature, breaking when brushed up against. It's the brittlebush plant. Externally it is frail, but internally it has a resin that makes it incredibly strong and resilient. It pictures the believer. Despite our frail estate that "breaks" easily in adversity, inwardly flows through the core of our being the sap of the Holy Spirit (brittlebush resin) that is able to hold our life together when it's falling apart. Lean into and rely upon the Holy Spirit and His power to sustain you in the worst of trials and sorrows.

Fear not, I am with thee, O be not dismayed,
For I am thy God, and will still give thee aid;
I'll strengthen thee, help thee, and cause thee to stand,
Upheld by My righteous, omnipotent hand.
~ George Keith (1787)

14   Unfailing Support

"Let the thought of His special love to you be a spiritual painkiller, a dear quietus to your woe."[91] ~ C. H. Spurgeon

What do we do when something happens that just doesn't make sense? We trust God, who says, "I will help thee" ("helper, assistant, i.e., one who assists and serves another with what is needed"[92]) your infirmities and adversities (Psalm 41:10). The term denotes that when our burden is too heavy to bear in our own strength, God promises to take hold of it at the opposite end and bear it with us.[93] That which is too heavy a load for us most assuredly is not for Him (Jeremiah 32:17 and Mark 9:23).

Have you ever tried to bear your burdens
        All alone? All alone?
Don't you know there's One Who waits to help you,
        Who will make all your burdens His own?

When I have burdens to bear which no one can share,
        I take them to Jesus, the Man of Calvary;
When I have crosses to bear, my Savior is there
        And always takes the heavy end and gives the light
            to me.
~ C. Austin Miles (1915)

Oswald Chambers wrote, "Commit to God whatever burden He has placed upon you. Don't just cast it aside, but put it over onto Him and place yourself there with it. You will see that your burden is then lightened by the sense of the companionship."

15 The Everlasting Arms

"He upholds the soul. Has the believer trials to come through? He is upheld to bear them. Has he temptations to face? He is upheld to conquer in them. Has he work to do? He is upheld and strengthened to perform it. Has he enemies to fight? His courage is sustained, and he is made 'more than conqueror.' But for the upholding of the 'everlasting arms,' how many of God's saints would never have come through what they have experienced!"[94]
~ J. Orr

What do we do when something happens that just doesn't make sense? We trust God to uphold us (Isaiah 41:10), preventing our fall into doubt, despair and manic depression. Underneath us are "the everlasting arms" of God (Deuteronomy 33:27). No clearer or more concise picture of the believer's security in God is found in all of Scripture. Their safeguard and hope rests not in feeble, frail and wavering faith, but in the everlasting clasp of His arms.

The everlasting arms of God can never be broken; they will forever hold firmly the child of God. In times of weakness and weariness, sickness and sorrow, the everlasting arms of God will prevent tottering in doubt and fear, while providing strength and comfort to endure. John Brown said, "I am weak, but it is delightful to feel oneself in the everlasting arms."[95] "The security of the saint is rooted in the fact that God has a hold of him, and not at all in his consciousness that he has a hold of God. His comfort may be affected by the latter, but his safety is due entirely to the former."[96]

What a fellowship, what a joy divine,
    Leaning on the everlasting arms!
What a blessedness, what a peace is mine,
    Leaning on the everlasting arms!
    ~ Elisha Albright Hoffman (1887)

16   *Blindsightedness*

"But when you pass through your own fiery trials and find God to be true to what He says, you have real help to offer others. What you are experiencing from God, you can give away in increasing measure to others."[97] ~ John Piper and Justin Taylor

What do we do when something happens that just doesn't make sense? We don't look at it from the vantage point of ourselves, but that of its being a benefit to others. Sometimes that which befalls us (changes, crisis, calamity) is purposed for the good of another.

Gardeners remove a plant not because of its need of being moved, but because it blocks the sunlight and air from getting to another near it.[98] God likewise at times works "strangely" toward us in order to shield those we love from harm and bring about their best good. He 'guides his hands wittingly.'[99]

He is "wonderful in counsel, and excellent in working" (Isaiah 28:29). "As for God, His way is perfect" (Psalm 18:30). At times, that which happens to us doesn't make sense because we fail to understand it may be happening for the benefit of others.

Christ's suffering and death on the Cross seemed senseless (for He was perfect and needed no atonement), until we understand it was ordained for the good of others (salvation, eternal life, Heaven, abundant life, etc.). Recall that Jesus said of the man blind from birth that "neither hath this man sinned, nor his parents: but that the works of God should be made manifest in him" (John 9:3). When including the good of others in the equation of our sufferings and troubles, the feeling of the senselessness of them is thwarted.

Not now, but in the coming years,
    It may be when with Christ we stand,
We'll read the meaning of our tears;
    And there, sometime, we'll understand.

We'll know why clouds instead of sun
     Were over many a cherished plan,
Why song has ceased when scarce begun.
     'Tis then, sometime, we'll understand.

Then trust in God through all thy days;
     Fear not, for He doth hold thy hand.
Though dark thy way, still sing and praise;
     Sometime, sometime, we'll understand.
       ~ James McGranahan (1840–1907)

17 The Tapestry of Life

"All that is made seems planless to the darkened mind, because there are more plans than it looked for."[100] ~ C. S. Lewis

What do we do when something happens that just doesn't make sense? We find comfort in knowing that God sees the "Big Picture," even when we cannot, and has everything in control. John Blanchard said, "Biblical patience is not rooted in fatalism that says everything is out of control. It is rooted in faith that says everything is in God's control."

Life may be viewed as a tapestry. Looking at its backside, only threads of various colors in a maze of confusion are seen. It's only when it's flipped over that its colors are seen blended together, forming a beautiful picture. In Heaven, the full, magnificent, beautiful tapestry will be seen, making clear the "why" of its particular weaving to the understanding and satisfaction of every grief-stricken believer. "We will understand it better by and by."

God knows the way; He holds the key;
     He guides us with unerring hand.
Sometime with tearless eyes we'll see;
     Yes, then, 'tis then, we'll understand.
       ~ James McGranahan (1840–1907)

A time will come when the unexplained things of life are clarified and the hard, disturbing questions answered, and the blurred will become unclouded and clear. Paul wrote, "In the same way, we can see and understand only a little about God now, as if we were peering at his reflection in a poor mirror; but someday we are going to see him in his completeness, face-to-face. Now all that I know is hazy and blurred, but then I will see everything clearly, just as clearly as God sees into my heart right now" (1 Corinthians 13:12 TLB). Spurgeon said, "It is natural for us to want to know, but we shall not know as we are known till we are present with the Lord. We are at school now; we shall go soon to the great university of Heaven and take our degree there."[101]

My life is but a weaving
    Between my God and me.
I cannot choose the colors
    He weaveth steadily.

Oft' times He weaveth sorrow,
    And I in foolish pride
Forget He sees the upper
    And I the underside.

Not 'til the loom is silent
    And the shuttles cease to fly,
Will God unroll the canvas
    And reveal the reason why.

The dark threads are as needful
    In the weaver's skillful hand
As the threads of gold and silver
    In the pattern He has planned.

He knows; He loves; He cares.
    Nothing this truth can dim.
He gives the very best to those
    Who leave the choice to Him.
      ~ Grant Colfax Tullar (1869–1950)

"By His omnipotence He rules in the world of mind as well as matter, and all things happen as He ordains."[102] For the moment trust the unseen Big Picture in the hands of Sovereign God who promises that every weave in the tapestry, good and bad, will work (blend) together for the believers best good (Romans 8:28).

18   Talk to Yourself

"As the wheelhouse and the steering gear and the rudder of the ship proclaim their purpose of guidance and direction, so eloquently and unmistakably does the make of our inward selves tell us that emotions and moods and tempers are meant to be governed, often to be crushed, always to be moderated, by sovereign will and reason."[103] ~ Alexander Maclaren

What do we do when something happens that just doesn't make sense? We talk to ourselves with wisdom and biblical conviction like David, who declared, "Why art thou cast down, O my soul? and why art thou disquieted within me? Hope in God." (Psalm 43:5). The Psalmist, in a state of mental anguish and gloom, arouses himself through self-interrogation not to fret but to trust in God for relief and consolation.

J. M. Boice states, "It is a case of the mind speaking to the emotions, rather than the emotions dictating to the mind."[104] D. Martyn Lloyd-Jones said, "You have to take yourself in hand; you have to address yourself, preach to yourself, question yourself. You must say to your soul, 'Why art thou cast down'—what business have you to be disquieted? You must turn on yourself, upbraid yourself, condemn yourself, exhort yourself, and say to yourself, 'Hope thou in God'—instead of muttering in this depressed, unhappy way."[105]

Talk to yourself like David did to himself (Psalm 43:5a) about the anxiety, in an effort to talk yourself out of it, as he did (Psalm 43:5b). Discipline the mind to bring "into captivity every thought to the obedience of Christ" (2 Corinthians 10:5). Talk yourself out of accepting the lies and devastating innuendos of Satan by meditation upon the truth of God's Word.

19 God Is Active When He Seems Idle

"The deep meaning of the Cross of Christ is that there is no suffering on earth that is not borne by God."[106] ~ Dietrich Bonhoeffer

What do we do when something happens that just doesn't make sense, when God seems distant, inactive, silent and unconcerned? You don't doubt His love or presence. Octavius Winslow admonishes, "Oh, deem not that Christ's love has chilled or changed towards you because He answers you not a word! He has loved you, O believer, from everlasting! He loves you still, and will love you unto the end! Wait in faith and patience; Jesus will break the silence—Christ will speak, the tempest shall subside, the clouds shall vanish, and sweet the peace your Father will give."[107] Saith Spurgeon, "Though we do not see His form bending over us nor mark the lovely light of those eyes that once were red with weeping, though we touch not that hand which felt the nails and hear no soft footfalls of the feet that were fastened to the cross, yet are we inwardly as certainly conscious of the shadow of Christ falling upon us as ever were His disciples when He stood in the tempest-tossed vessel and said to winds and waves, 'Peace, be still.'"[108]

> The people of God in the day of affliction are not abandoned by God. He is nigh when He seems absent. He is watching when He seems blind. He is active when He seems idle.
> G. Campbell Morgan

In Jesus' physical absence from Bethany (when Lazarus was sick), He was yet there orchestrating all that happened for His greater glory and Mary and Martha's best good. The unseen hand of Christ starts to work at the first cry of desperation, only later to be evidenced visibly. In the silences of Christ there are unknown divine intentions and designs at play (as was the case with Mary and Martha). See John 11:1–6. G. Campbell Morgan said, "The people of God in the day of affliction are not abandoned by God. He is nigh when He seems absent. He is watching when He seems blind. He is active when He seems idle."[109]

Our Christian forefathers spoke of "spiritual desertion" —the sense of divine abandonment. But despite what their emotions testified, the promises of God affirm that shall never be the case for the child of God (James 4:8). Zephaniah said, "The LORD your God is in your midst, A victorious warrior. He will exult over you with joy, He will be quiet in his love, He will rejoice over you with shouts of joy" (Zephaniah 3:17 NASB 1995). The prophet makes clear that God exults over us in joy even when He is "quiet in His love." Saith Randy Alcorn, "Many of us have walked the Emmaus Road (Luke 24:13–32). Overwhelmed by sorrow, plagued by questions, we wonder where God is, when all along, He walks beside us."[110]

Interpret the silences of Christ with the backdrop of Calvary, and the heart will remain calm. To quote Winslow again, "God's silence to you in this overwhelming calamity, in this crushing affliction, in this overshadowing cloud, in this bitter trial, is the silence of infinite and unchangeable love. Wait, and He will speak anon; and sweet, assuring, and soothing will be the words that shall break that silence, the stillness of which has filled your mind with forebodings so painful and with an awe so profound: 'It is I, do not be afraid!' Your bounding heart shall respond, 'It is the voice of my Beloved!'"[111] In the inexplicable storms, discipline yourself to wait silently upon and for God (Psalm 62:1). With all murmuring, complaining, speculating and questioning silenced, await God to speak peace and calm to your soul.

20   The Anchor Holds

"Many a text [of Scripture] is written in a secret ink which must be held to the fire of adversity to make it visible."[112] ~ C. H. Spurgeon

What do we do when something happens that just doesn't make sense? We remain anchored to His Word and promises. We grip tightly His inerrant Word and cling to its unfailing promises. David said, "Unless thy law had been my delights, I should then have perished in mine affliction" (Psalm 119:92). That is, David would have been overcome, discouraged and defeated by the heavy weight of his burden and sorrow had it not been for God's Word and its promises to sustain him (uphold him). In times of the unexplainable, hide in the refuge of His Word, declaring with great earnestness and confidence, 'Lord, You are my hiding place and my shield. My hope is based on Your Word' (Psalm 119:114).

The renowned hymn "Standing on the Promises of God" was written by Russell Carter. It took the diagnosis of a critical heart condition (age 30) and possible imminent death for him, however, to understand what it meant to rest on God's promises. Carter knelt and made a promise to God that whether He healed him or not, his life forever would be dedicated to His work. It was from that moment forward that the Holy Scriptures took on new meaning for Carter and he began to lean on the promises that he had wrote about previously in the hymn he composed. He chose to believe them, regardless of whether or not God granted him healing. He was healed and lived for another 49 years as an instrument of God's grace.[113] May we but follow his worthy example.

Standing [trusting] on the promises that cannot fail.
When the howling storms of doubt and fear assail,
By the living Word of God I shall prevail—
Standing on the promises of God.
~ Russell Kelso Carter (1886)

In the time of adversity or infirmity when the body is weak and the mind is feeble, we are prone to forget the truths and promises of God's Word that instill comfort. It is by the enabling of the Holy Spirit, the Holy Comforter, that such things are recalled when needed the most.[114] The Word of God, the anchor of our faith, will hold despite the fierceness of the storm (Hebrews 6:19). Matthew

Henry says, "He will take us by the hand as our guide, to lead us in our way, will help us up when we are fallen or prevent our falls; when we are weak, He will hold us up; wavering, He will fix us; trembling, He will encourage us."[115]

21   Don't Give Place to the Devil

"That man is perfect in faith who can come to God in the utter dearth of his feelings and desires; without a glow or an aspiration; with the weight of low thoughts, failures, neglects, and wandering forgetfulness, and say to Him, 'Thou art my refuge.'"[116] ~ George MacDonald

What do we do when something happens that just doesn't make sense? We give no place to the Devil to work doubt and fear in our mind (Ephesians 4:27). As A. W. Tozer says, learn to talk back to the Devil. Rebuke in Jesus' name Satan's lies, taunting, innuendos, and intimidations (John 8:44). Don't give place to them. Don't flee your tower of refuge and Guardian Protector for an unprotected foxhole. Guard your thoughts; protect the mind from the injurious arrows of doubt shot from the bow of Satan (Ephesians 6:17). "Trials should not surprise us or cause us to doubt God's faithfulness."[117]

The Word of God is a retardant to the fiery darts of accusations of the deceiver, so stay much in it. Charles Hodge said, "In opposition...to all the suggestions of the Devil, the sole, simple, and sufficient answer is the Word of God. This puts to flight all the powers of darkness. The Christian finds this to be true in his individual experience. It dissipates his doubts; it drives away his fears; it delivers him from the power of Satan."[118] John MacArthur says that the only statement in the Bible about winning against Satan boils down to submitting to God and resisting the Devil. If we do that, Satan has to flee from us (James 4:7).[119]

22 It Is God That Worketh

"When God puts His own people into the furnace, He keeps His eye on the clock and His hand on the thermostat. He knows how long and how much. We may question why He does it to begin with, or why He doesn't turn down the heat or even turn it off; but our questions are only evidences of unbelief."[120] ~ Warren Wiersbe

What do we do when something happens that just doesn't make sense? We rely upon the fact that "it is God which worketh ['to energize, to work effectively'[121]] in you, both to will and to do of his good pleasure" (Philippians 2:13). James McConkey writes, "When He leads you into paths that wound your faltering feet, confronts you with a future that lowers dark and threatening, hems you in with providence that seem harsh and mysterious—in all these stand still; whisper to yourself, 'It is God that worketh,' and TRUST Him. It matters not that His dealings with you are strange, mysterious, even confusing; that this is not the way in which you would like Him to work. You may not indeed understand all this, but *He does,* 'for it is God that worketh in you.' But you would not dare take your case out of His hands even if you could—would you? Therefore, trust Him while He in you works. He must purify the gold ere He send it forth as sterling coin, the choicest of His mintage."[122] See Isaiah 48:10.

Charles Simeon said, "Thus we see that the weakest Christian stands on a rock which defies all the storms and tempests that ever can assail it. Let us then 'be strong in the Lord, and in the power of his might' and look to Him to fulfil in us all 'the good pleasure of his will.'"[123] Spurgeon says, "The wisdom and power of the great Workman are discovered by the trials through which His vessels of mercy are permitted to pass."[124] W. A. Criswell states, "The providential trials of our life are to make true sons of us, to reveal the gold of God that is in us—a refiner's fire."[125]

23 Blame the Devil

"Satan can never be content till he sees the believer utterly devoured. He would rend him in pieces and break his bones and utterly destroy him, if he could. Do not, therefore, indulge the thought that the main purpose of Satan is to make you miserable."[126] ~ C. H. Spurgeon

What do we do when something happens that just doesn't make sense? At times its justified to blame the bizarre and unfair trials of life upon Satan and the demons of Hell, allowed by God for a designed purpose. "Satan and his demons never, never act against God's people," writes John MacArthur, "without the permission of God. And when God gives them permission, He always uses their work to accomplish some divine purpose. Often, to exalt the power of God and prove the devotion of His followers, God permits Satan to work the hardest on the noblest servants of God."[127] God allowed Satan (removed the hedge of protection about Job) to test righteous Job maliciously and mercilessly to prove that Job was an upright and just man that loved Him supremely (Job 1:8–12).

Upon being granted permission to test Job, Satan immediately found willing helpers (Sabeans—Job 1:15; and Chaldeans—Job 1:17) to do exactly his bidding. Even nature was subject to his control (winds—Job 1:19; lightning strikes—Job 1:16). Job lost his family (all but his wife), possessions, and health. But Job prevailed against Satan because God never ceased to be in control and protective of him through the entire bizarre ordeal, although it may have seemed otherwise. Saith Spurgeon, "Did not the Lord also consider how he should sustain his servant under the trial? Beloved, you do not know how blessedly our God poured the secret oil upon Job's fire of grace while the Devil was throwing buckets of water on it. He saith to Himself, 'If Satan shall do much, I will do more; if he takes away much, I will give more; if he tempts the man to curse, I will fill him so full of love to Me that he shall bless Me. I will help him; I will strengthen him; yea, I will uphold him with the right hand of My righteousness. Christian, take those two thoughts and put them under your tongue as a wafer made with honey."[128]

However dark the trial or fierce the storm Satan is allowed to thrust upon us, we are more than conquerors through Christ who died and rose again. That which Joseph said of his brothers, the believer surely may say regarding the inflictions of Satan, "You meant to hurt [to harm; or evil against] me, but God turned your evil into [meant it for] good" (Genesis 50:20 EXB). Christopher Ash writes, "[The] assurance that God can do all things and that no purpose of His can be thwarted is the comfort I need in suffering and the encouragement I crave when terrified by evil. He does not merely permit evil, but commands it, controls it, and uses it for His good purposes. [The] God who knows how to use supernatural evil to serve His purposes of ultimate good can and will use the darkest invasion of my life for His definite and invincible plans for my good in Christ."[129]

24   A Fortress Impregnable

"My soul is utterly frantic for that single place of perfect refuge from which I can clearly see the winds rip and hear the tempest tear, yet despite the ferocity of the tumult I rest in such a sublime peace it is as if neither existed at all. And if I have not yet found such a place, it is because I have not yet found God."[130] ~ Craig D. Lounsbrough

What do we do when something happens that just doesn't make sense and for which there is no good explanation? The safe recourse is to flee to the impregnable fortress of God's safety. "He will dwell on the heights, His refuge will be the impregnable rock; His bread will be given him, His water will be sure" (Isaiah 33:16 NASB). Some attribute the words about Hezekiah, others to Christ, but I see them applicable to the child of God. God will be our impregnable fortress in the time of storm and battle. Solomon therefore said, "The name of the LORD is a strong tower: the righteous runneth into it, and is safe" (Proverbs

18:10). "*We* may be assaulted both by men and devils; but *we* are assured, that 'God will keep *us* by His own power, through faith.'"[131] Adam Clarke states, "The Lord is round about His people—He is above, beneath, around them; and while they keep within it, their fortress is impregnable, and they can suffer no evil."[132]

When darkness veils His lovely face,
I'll rest on His unchanging grace.
In every high and stormy day,
My anchor holds within the veil.

On Christ the solid rock I stand.
All other ground is sinking sand;
All other ground is sinking sand.
~ Edward Mote (1834)

25 God Is for You

"If your soul is written upon the palms of Jesus' hands, and engraved on His heart, no weapon which is formed against you shall prosper."[133] ~ C. H. Spurgeon

What do we do when something happens that just doesn't make sense? Accept the fact that God is on your side. Martin Luther poignantly taught that "suffering is unbearable if you aren't certain that God is for you and with you."[134] And he is correct. The Bible says, "For the LORD your God is he that goeth with you, to fight for you against your enemies, to save you" (Deuteronomy 20:4). The Lord is on your side. He hasn't abandoned you or set Himself against you as an enemy. Despite what seems to be, God is for you and with you. Though the infirmity or affliction seems insurmountable, God is on your side. Though the grief is almost impossible to bear, God is on your side. Though others may have forsaken you, God is on your side. Though the situation provides no rational explanation, God is for you and with you. Though there appears to be no way out, God is on your side. Though the burden is heavier than you can possibly bear, God is on your side. Though your circumstance looks hopeless, God is on your side. And because Almighty God is on your side, He will sustain you through all that devastates and causes despair. Paul argues, "What shall we then say to these things? If God be for us, who can be against us?" (Romans 8:31).

Spurgeon says, "He was for us before the worlds were made. He was for us, or else He never would have given His Son. He was for us even when He smote the only begotten and laid the whole weight of His wrath upon Him— He was for us, though He was against Him. He was for us when we were ruined in the fall—He loved us notwithstanding all. He was for us when we were against Him and with a high hand were bidding Him defiance. He was for us, or else He never would have brought us humbly to seek His face. He has been for us in many struggles; we have had to fight through multitudes of difficulties; we have had temptations from without and within—how could we have held on until now if He had not been with us? He is for us, let me say, with all the infinity of His heart, with all the omnipotence of His love, for us with all His boundless wisdom; arrayed in all the attributes which make Him God He is for us—eternally and immutably for us, for us when yon blue skies shall be rolled up like a worn-out vesture, for us throughout eternity. Here, child of God, is matter enough for thought, even though you had ages to meditate upon it: God is for you, and if God be for you, who can be against you?"[135]

And with God for us, there is no mountain that cannot be climbed, no river that cannot be crossed, no opposition that cannot be thwarted, and no problem that cannot be solved. He says, "For I am the LORD your God who takes hold of your right hand and says to you, Do not fear; I will help you" (Isaiah 41:13 NIV). Never take a step without saying, "I've got this, for God is on my side to enable me to undertake it victoriously.

26   *Just Hang On to God*

"One reason many people never see God working in their lives is because they never hang in long enough for God to show His power."[136] ~ Wayne Styles

What do we do when something happens that just doesn't make sense? We hang tightly to the hand of God. The Bible says, "They that trust in the Lord shall be as mount Zion, which cannot be removed, but abideth forever" (Psalm 125:1). Alexander Maclaren says the word "trust" "literally means to 'hang upon' something, and so, beautifully, it tells us what faith is—just hanging upon God."[137] In the time of trouble, hang on to the sovereign hand of God that will not let you go. Matthew Henry said, "All that deal with God must deal upon trust, and He will give comfort to those only that give credit to Him and make it to appear they do so by quitting other confidences."[138]

Within Thy circling power I stand;
On every side I find Thy hand.
Awake, asleep, at home, abroad,
I am surrounded still with God.
          ~ Isaac Watts (1856)

Martin Luther wrote, "It is much easier to learn than to believe that we who have by us the Word of God and receive it are surrounded with divine aid. If we were surrounded by walls of steel and fire, we should feel secure and defy the Devil. But the property of faith is not to be proud of what the eye sees, but to rely on what the Word reveals."[139] "It's not important that I have an explanation from God for the 'furnace'; it is sufficient to know that He is with me in it and will see me through it."[140]

27 Praying Makes a Difference

"Our prayers do make a difference."[141] ~ Max Lucado

What do we do when something happens that just doesn't make sense? We don't quit praying for discernment, conquest (deliverance), and comfort. "We pray," Oswald Chambers says, "when there's nothing else we can do; Jesus wants us to pray before we do anything at all."[142] Spurgeon states, "Let your cares drive you to God. I shall not mind if you have many of them if each one leads you to prayer. If every fret makes you lean more on the Beloved, it will be a benefit."[143] Ron Dunn said, "Prayer is like a missile. It can fly at the speed of thought. It can reach any target anywhere, and there is no anti-ballistic missile that can shoot it down."[144]

> It is that communion with God which renders us impervious to midnight frights and horrors born of darkness.
>
> C. H. Spurgeon

Grasp this truth from the pen of E. M. Bounds firmly. "The man that truly prays gets from God things denied the prayerless man."[145] The Bible says, "Ye have not, because ye ask not" (James 4:2), and, "This is the confidence that we have in him, that, if we ask any thing according to His will, he heareth us" (1 John 5:14). Adrian Rogers states, "Prayer is laying hold of God's will. The only thing that lies outside the reach of prayer is that which lies outside the will of God. There are things God has for you that will only come about if you pray."[146] "So the first thing we ought to do when we hurt," says Rogers, "is pray, 'Lord, take it away, please.' If He doesn't, ask Him again, and continue to ask Him until He tells you that He has a better or a higher plan."[147]

In days of deepest anxiety, pain and confusion, when prayers seem not to penetrate the skies and seem to meet with no response, we must pray on. When it's the hardest thing to do to pray, pray the hardest. Obviously, prayer may be simply denied, thus unanswered (unbiblical prayer or prayer outside His will). Answer to other prayers may be delayed. Adrian Rogers explains, "With God, timing is far more important than time."[148] Prayer may be delayed to dispense His grace, display His glory or to give something better than requested.[149]

Matthew Henry states, "Cast not away your confidence because God defers His performances. That which does not come in your time will be hastened in His time, which is always the more convenient season. God will work when He pleases, how He pleases, and by what means He pleases. He is not bound to keep our time, but He will perform His word, honor our faith, and reward them that diligently seek Him."[150]

Though He may delay His response, it is always on time. Thomas Watson says, "God cannot deny a praying soul."[151] Woodrow Kroll says, "Fervent prayers produce phenomenal results."[152] Perseverance in prayer is rewarded with an answer. God unites importunate praying with answered prayer.[153] See Luke 18:1. "It is that communion with God," states Spurgeon, "which renders us impervious to midnight frights and horrors born of darkness."[154]

Keep on praying to God on high.
Keep on praying; He hears your cry.
God will answer the sincere heart.
Keep on praying; He will do His part.
         ~ F. W. Vandersloot (1906)

28 The Night-Counsel of the Lord

"My eyes anticipate the night watches, That I may meditate on Your word." ~ Psalm 119:148 NASB 1995

What do we do when something happens that just doesn't make sense, that keeps us tossing and turning, unable to sleep at night? We turn our pillow into an altar and allow God to instruct us, as did David who, when facing death, said, "I will bless the Lord who counsels me; he gives me wisdom in the night. He tells me what to do" (Psalm 16:7 TLB). David found the "night seasons," when others were sleeping, opportune times to consult with the Lord and meditate. He testifies, "When I remember Thee upon my bed, and meditate on Thee in the night watches" (Psalm 63:6); and, "In the middle of the night, I get up to thank you because your laws are so fair" (Psalm 119:62 ERV). See Psalm 42:8; 77:6; 4:4.

The word rendered "night" or "night watches" is in the plural, which reveals it was a customary time for meditation and communion with God for David. J. S. Perowne paraphrases David's words in this fashion (Psalm 16:7): "God has led me to find my joy in Him, and now in the night seasons, as the time most favorable to quiet thought, I meditate thereon."[155] "He preferred study to slumber, and he learned to forgo his necessary sleep for much more necessary devotion. It is instructive to find meditation so constantly connected with fervent prayer. It is the fuel which sustains the flame."[156]

Allen Harman says, "True meditation is never with a blank mind, but is based on God's revealed Word."[157] New hope is engendered and peace found. Saith Spurgeon, "The communion of the soul with God brings to it an inner spiritual wisdom which in still seasons is revealed to itself."[158] Look to God for "Night Counsel," as David did, and experience His touch of comfort, consolation, peace, grace, and strength to bear this difficult trial and ordeal.

29 *Spurgeon's Secret of Coping*

"I believe the promises of God enough to venture an eternity on them."[159] ~ Isaac Watts

What do we do when something happens that just doesn't make sense? We do what the great British pastor of London, C. H. Spurgeon, did when smitten with cruel gout and kidney disease. We lean heavy into the promises of God for hope, comfort, clarification, and consolation.

It was during his time of intense suffering physically and mentally that he began the writing of the devotional *Cheque Book of the Bank of Faith.* "I commenced these daily portions when I was wading in the surf of controversy. Since then, I have been cast into 'waters to swim in,' which, but for God's upholding hand, would have proved waters to drown in. I have endured tribulation from many flails. Sharp bodily pain suc-ceeded mental depression, and this was accompanied both by bereavement, and affliction in the person of one dear as life [Susannah]. The waters rolled in continually, wave upon wave. I do not mention this to exact sympathy, but simply to let the reader see that I am no dry-land sailor. I have traversed those oceans which are not Pacific full many a time; I know the roll of the billows and the rush of the winds. Never were the promises of Jehovah so precious to me as at this hour. Some of them I never understood till now; I had not reached the date at which they matured, for I was not myself mature enough to perceive their meaning."[160]

Later he wrote, "How much more wonderful is the Bible to me now than it was a few months ago! I have not received new promises; but the result to me is much the same as if I had done so, for the old ones have opened up to me with richer stores."[161]

When the unexplainable happens, lean heavy into the promises of God. Claim the promises. Cling to the promises. Confide in the promises. Capitulate to the promises. And find calm and comfort in the promises. Make thy stay in that hour the precious promises of God, and peace and solace will be your gain. As with Spurgeon, the old promises will open up with heavenly nectar never seen before, to grant sustenance, hope and comfort.

He promised to keep me, support and defend me,
    When trials o'ertake and temptations assail.
He promised to guide me; and I am persuaded
    His promises never, no, never can fail.

Onward I journey; no need shall I know
    But that His goodness and power will bestow.
The while I am clinging, my glad heart is singing;
    For Christ is beside me wherever I go.
        ~ William C. Poole (1912)

With Spurgeon, you may freely take any promise contained in Holy Scriptures and say, "Lord, fulfil this word unto thy servant whereon thou hast caused me to hope"[162] [Psalm 119:49], and it shall be so. Come and trust Him to do that which He has pledged.

30 Bad Things Happen to Good People

"I am learning that mature faith, which encompasses both simple faith and fidelity, works the opposite of paranoia. It reassembles all the events of life around trust in a loving God. When good things happen, I accept them as gifts from God, worthy of thanksgiving. When bad things happen, I do not take them as necessarily sent by God—I see evidence in the Bible to the contrary—and I find in them no reason to divorce God. Rather, I trust that God can use even those bad things for my benefit."[163] ~ Philip Yancey

What do we do when something happens that just doesn't make sense? We understand that the godliest are not exempt from bizarre, mysterious and unfair things. They happened to Job. The Bible states that he "worshiped God and was faithful to him. He was a good man, careful not to do anything evil" (Job 1:1 GNT). Job's story demolishes the notion that we can avoid turmoil, calamity, disease and hardship if we're walking in fellowship with the Lord. No one was godlier or more spiritual than Job (Job 1:8).

In my early ministry, a ministerial friend taught that bad things happened to good people because of their moral failure or other acts of disobedience. Though biblically true (chastisement, Hebrews 12:7–9), it is far from always being the case or the norm. Sometimes bad things happen to good people for the same reason as they did to Job—to put their faith and allegiance to God to the test and prove their unwavering trust in God and love to Him. At times, bad things happen to mature the saint, develop his spiritual muscles and purify his heart more toward the Lord. At times bad things are allowed to happen to the believer for the sake of the kingdom (family, friends, comrades in the faith, and the advancement of His cause). And sometimes, bad things are allowed to happen to good people to put on display for God's honor and glory His miraculous power to sustain His own in the darkest of nights and deepest of trials. We are learning that praying for God's protection is not equal to praying for His best good, for often that which is best for us and our loved ones and His glory entails hardship, suffering, sorrow and the unexplainables. This is why bad things happen to good people.

Spurgeon says, "Job did not understand the Lord's reasons [for the hardship and pain], but he continued to confide in His goodness. He set no terms or limits to the Lord's action, but left all to His absolute will, and was sure that whatever He might do it must be right."[164] The bad experienced by some believers will remain a "mystery" until later. These precious saints must embrace Job's attitude, for the reason for his suffering was a mystery to him. He said, "Though He slay me, yet will I trust in him" (Job 13:15).

31 *Trusting God Is a Choice, Not a Feeling*

"I have complete confidence that God is able to take care of any situation and provide an answer to any question or problem — He has all the resources of the universe to draw upon in helping each one of us through any type of crisis, if we will trust Him."[165]
~ Charles Stanley

What do we do when something happens that just doesn't make sense? We mentally choose to trust God instead of relying upon tenuous feelings and frail emotions which are unreliable, undependable, and unpredictable.

Factual trust in God's faithfulness to care for His children is the opposite; it's based upon God's track record cited in Scripture, His sure and sufficient promises, and the testimonials of the saints over the centuries. Faith is choosing to believe God over negative feelings and human perception.

Elizabeth Elliot said, "Faith is not an instinct. It certainly is not a feeling—feelings don't help much when you're in the lion's den or hanging on a wooden Cross. Faith is not inferred from the happy way things always work. It is an act of the will, a choice, based on the unbreakable Word of a God who cannot lie and who showed us what love and obedience and sacrifice mean, in the person of Jesus Christ."[166]

Jesus taught the value of faith over feeling in the story of the two houses that battled intense storms (Matthew 7:24–28). In essence He said that the foundation of feeling ("sand") is not to be trusted to sustain us when the rain descends upon the house. It's incapable of bearing the infliction it brings and will crash to the ground (Matthew 7:26–27). But on the other hand, the foundation of faith ("solid rock," firm trust in God despite the intensity of the storm battling the house) is the believers' sure and steady hope, enabling the house to withstand the storm victoriously (Matthew 7:25). The difference between survival and defeat in the fierce storms of life is the foundation on which life is based. Spurgeon said, "You may readily judge whether you are a child of God or a hypocrite by seeing in what direction your soul turns in seasons of severe trial. The hypocrite flies to the world and finds a sort of comfort there. But the child of God runs to his Father and expects consolation only from the Lord's hand."[167]

When the music suddenly stops and darkness fills the skies and the spring turns to bitter winter, when the love of life has been silenced and painful senseless things happen that perplex and baffle, our only recourse is trust in God. We pray with Andrew Murray, *"Mighty God, I claim thy almightiness,"*[168] for it will be His omnipotence only that will sustain us.

Other refuge have I none;
        Hangs my helpless soul on Thee.
Leave, oh, leave me not alone;
        Still support and comfort me.

All my trust on Thee is stayed;
        All my help from Thee I bring.
Cover my defenseless head
        With the shadow of Thy wing.
                    ~ Charles Wesley (1740)

Amidst the unexplainable adversities of life, *choose to say* with Habakkuk, "Although the fig tree shall not blossom, neither shall fruit be in the vines; the labor of the olive shall fail, and the fields shall yield no meat; the flock shall be cut off from the fold, and there shall be no herd in the stalls: Yet I will rejoice in the LORD, I will joy in the God of my salvation. The LORD God is my strength, and he will make my feet like hinds' feet, and he will make me to walk upon mine high places" (Habakkuk 3:17–19).

32 No More Than I Can Bear

"God will never make you take even one step beyond what your feet are able to endure. Never mind if you think you are unable to take another step, for either He will strengthen you to make you able, or He will call a sudden halt, and you will not have to take it at all."[169] ~ Frances Ridley Havergal

What do we do when something happens that just doesn't make sense, a something that seems beyond our ability to withstand? We trust God not to put on us more than we can bear.

Paul writes, "We want you to know, Christian brothers, of the trouble we had in the countries of Asia. The load was so heavy we did not have the strength to keep going. At times we did not think we could live. We thought we would die. This happened so we would not put our trust in ourselves, but in God Who raises the dead" (2 Corinthians 1:8–9 NLV).

Tony Evans said, "In order to take Paul deeper in faith, God put him in a situation that his résumé, abilities, and connections could not change. Why? So that Paul would learn to trust God through experiencing Him more fully."[170]

It is wrong to say that God will not put on us more than we can bear. Paul's experience testifies that such may happen. (First Corinthians 10:13 refers to sinful temptations, particularly sexual immorality and idolatry, not hardships). However, it is right to say that God will not put on us more hardship or infirmity than we can bear with His assistance (Philippians 4:13). With Him in the equation, all things are bearable, endurable—yes, even your present grief that seems insurmountable and all the questions that presently that are unanswerable.

33 *Heavenly Lenses*

"We must learn to live on the heavenly side and look at things from above. To contemplate all things as God sees them, as Christ beholds them, overcomes sin, defies Satan, dissolves perplexities, lifts us above trials, separates us from the world, and conquers fear of death."[171] ~ A. B. Simpson

What are we to do when something happens that just doesn't make sense? We must look at it through the lens (perspective) of Heaven. The type of lenses through which we view events determines our interpretation of and response to them. Distorted lenses (finite knowledge and perspective, grief, anger, pain, fear) impede accurate comprehension of the mysterious working of a Sovereign God (Isaiah 55:8–9).

Perspective is "the capacity to view things in their true relations or relative importance."[172] A heavenly perspective sees what happens from God's vantage point and weighs them how He weighs them.

Joni Eareckson Tada said, "Looking down on my problems from Heaven's perspective, trials looked extraordinarily different. When viewed from its own lèvel, my paralysis seemed like a huge, impassable wall; but when viewed from above, the wall appeared as a thin line, something that could be overcome."[173] May God grant us lenses to view from Heaven's perspective that which is plaguing our life with pain, suffering, and sorrow. "Souls that soar to Heaven's heights on wings like eagles overcome the mud of earth that keeps us stuck to a temporal, limited perspective."[174] See Isaiah 40:31.

"The way to peace and victory is to accept every circumstance and every trial as being straight from the hand of our loving Father; to live 'with him in the heavenly realms' (Ephesians 2:6), above the clouds, in the very presence of His throne; and to look down from glory on our circumstances as being lovingly and divinely appointed."[175]

34 When All Seems Hopeless

"Hope means hoping when things are hopeless, or it is no virtue at all. As long as matters are really hopeful, hope is mere flattery or platitude; it is only when everything is hopeless that hope begins to be a strength."[176] ~ G. K. Chesterton

What do we do when something happens that just doesn't make sense? We stand firm, rooted in hope, refusing to give place to hard or bad thoughts about God. Paul exhorts, "Do all things [bear all things] without murmurings and disputings" (Philippians 2:14). John MacArthur comments that "complaining" [NLT] refers to muttering or grumbling in a low tone. "It is an emotional rejection of God's providence, will and circumstances for one's life. The word for 'disputing' is more intellectual and here means 'questionings' or 'criticisms' directed negatively toward God."[177]

The choicest of saints, in suffering, may encounter temptation to murmur against, doubt, question or criticize God (Hebrews 10:23). Job did. Satan said to God of Job,

"Touch all that he has, and he will curse You to Your face" (Job 1:11 AMPC). However, Job proved him wrong, saying, "Though He slay me ["Job included in his supposition all kinds of pain"[178]], yet I will trust in him" (Job 13:15). May we, like Job, refuse to mar our Lord's holy visage and nature by reason of grumbling amidst horrendous pain and grief.

In the sternest of storms, hope possessed in Christ will be the antidote to the derision of Satan and despair of soul, preventing stumbling. Hope says that we confidently can expect something to happen because God promised it would come to pass. Augustine said, "God is not a deceiver, that He should offer to support us, and then, when we lean upon Him, should slip away from us."[179] Hope is not wishful thinking, but certitude based upon God's unalterable promises. Hope grants enduring peace in trial, grief, illness and approaching death (Job 11:18). Hope is threaded with patience for that which is hoped for until it does come to pass (1 Thessalonians 1:3). Hope will not disappoint, for it rests in that which Christ accomplished at Calvary and His priestly role as our High Priest. Hope has as its foundation the promise of God that He will work good out of the believer's adversity and infirmity (Romans 8:28). The power of hope is not in the hope itself but in Christ's indisputable power to fulfill His promises with regard to the specific aspect of the hope. Hope will abide with the believer in every circumstance, and then as he forges the chilly Jordan into the Promised Land, it will prop him up. Spurgeon said, "Hope is one of the last blessings God gives us, and one that abides last with us."[180]

35 The Best Sermon to Preach to Self

"Through the dark and stormy night,
Faith beholds a feeble light
Up the blackness streaking;
Knowing God's own time is best,
In a patient hope I rest
For the full day-breaking!"[181] ~ John Greenleaf Whittier

What do we do when something happens that just doesn't make sense? We preach to ourselves. Hope at times must be summoned. Recall that David exhorted his own soul, saying, "Hope thou in God" (Psalm 42:5). The best sermon to preach to yourself is three words long: "Hope in God!" Do so forcefully and seriously. Hope is strengthened by trust (confidence) in God, that He is in absolute control of all that happens, and in the certainty and validity of His promises,.Spurgeon said, "I [would] like to see thee have a good long measuring-rod, when it is made of hope. Hope is a tall companion; he wades right through the sea and is not drowned. You cannot kill him, do what you may."[182] Hope and faith "can read love in the blackest of Divine dispensa-tion, as by a rainbow we see the beautiful image of the sun's light in the midst of a dark and waterish cloud."[183] David Wilkerson said, "Only God can shut out the waves of depression and feelings of loneliness and failure that come over you. Faith in God's love alone can salvage the hurt mind."[184]

When others ask how you reacted to adversity, let the resounding reply be, "As one that possessed a hope in the Lord Jesus Christ" (1 Thessalonians 4:13). George Müller said, "Oh, remember this: There is never a time when we may not hope in God. Whatever our necessities, however great our difficulties, and though to all appearance help is impossible, yet our business is to hope in God, and it will be found that it is not in vain. In the Lord's own time help will come."[185] See Psalm 33:22.

Thomas Goodwin said, "He is not only called the God of hope because He is the object of hope, but because He is the Author of it; and all the Scripture is written to work hope in us, saith verse 4 of the same chapter"[186] (Romans 15).

36   Cleave to Christ in Crisis

"It is not my love only that I am to fasten upon God, but my whole self that I am to bind to Him. God delights in us when we cling to Him."[187] ~ Alexander Maclaren

What do we do when something happens that doesn't make sense? We answer Peter's question: "Lord, to whom shall we go?" (John 6:68) with the same certitude as he did (v. 69). We cleave to Christ. Octavius Winslow says, "It is in cleaving by faith [to Christ] in the deep waters, and in climbing the difficult ascent, we reach the firmest footing, and the highest, brightest, holiest elevation in our Christianity—the complete absorption of our will in God's will."[188]

What do we do when the unreasonable and bizarre occurs? We say with the psalmist, "But it is good for me to draw near to God [cleave to Him]: I have put my trust in the Lord GOD" (Psalm 73:28). We are to pursue hope (John 6:68b–69); where may it be found but in Christ? We are to pursue peace (comfort in sorrow and suffering—Exodus 15:26, and tranquility in heart—John 14:27); where may it be known but in Christ, the *real* Peace-Giver? We are to pursue forgiveness (1 John 1:7); where may it be received but from Christ? We are to pursue happiness (John 10:10); where might it be attained but in Christ? We are to pursue Heaven (John 14:6); who can make it possible but Christ? If not to Christ, then to whom can we go to satisfy these cries of the heart? To philosophy, religion, the Mosaic Law, humanism, academia? Will we turn to "broken cisterns" instead of the "fountain of living waters" (Jeremiah 2:13)?

No, all but Christ are empty and frail to supply our need. He only is the Divine Redeemer, the Son of God capable of providing man with that which is needed in the sunshine and the rain, life and death (John 6:68). Horatius Bonar wrote, "To grieve, and yet have no comforter; to be wounded, and yet have no healer; to be weary, and yet know no resting-place—this is the world's hard lot. Yet it is a self-chosen one. GOD did not choose it for them. They chose it for themselves. [If to Him they come] He will satisfy their craving souls; He will turn their midnight into noon; He will give them beauty for ashes, the oil of joy for mourning, the garment of praise for the spirit of heaviness that they may be called trees of righteousness, the planting of the Lord."[189]

Hear God speak: "I am the LORD; there is no other god. I will give you the strength you need, although you do not know me" (Isaiah 45:5 GNT). With the certitude of Peter in the hour of the unexplainable and seemingly senseless, let us attest to Christ: "Thou hast the words of eternal life [promises of eternal life which point the way to salvation]. And we believe and are sure that thou art that Christ, the Son of the living God" (John 6:68b–69). Failure to do so is dangerous peril, filled with fear, anxiety and chaos.

37 *The Lord Is There*

"The Lord is there, to guard and hold his own."[190] ~ C. H. Spurgeon

What do we do when something happens that doesn't make sense? We never forget that God is Jehovah-Shammah, "The LORD is there" (Ezekiel 48:35). Wherever the "there" may be—arrival of good or bad news, illness, terminal disease, suffering, sorrow, hardship or approaching death—the Lord is "there."

He is there with the healing balm of Gilead, the comforting ministry of the Holy Spirit, the protection of holy angels (they are nearer than you believe), the nourishment and encouragement of His sacred promises, the support of the saints, and His own sweet presence. Though Jesus was there in Bethabara, He was yet there in Bethany ministering to Mary and Martha (John 11.5–6). Though in Palestine, He was there in the belly of the fish delivering Jonah (Jonah 2:10). Though there in Cana with the nobleman, He was there healing his son in Capernaum (John 4:50). Though there in the city of Capernaum with the centurion, He was there healing his paralyzed servant at his home some distance away (Matthew 8:13). And knowing that "the LORD is there" before we get "there," when we get "there," and will always be "there" through our "there," brings consolation and peace incomparable. The Christian may be embattled by various storms and venomous attacks of Satan, yet he will be perpetually preserved, for "the LORD is there." Though loved ones in deepest trial are somewhere over "there" out of our reach or ability to help, rest assured God is ministering to them in their "there."

Though the bush may burn (as in the wilderness with Moses), because He is there, it will not be consumed. The bottom line is that God's "there" is everywhere and anywhere His children need Him, even in the hard-to-understand circumstances of life. And though He may be silent, His presence unseen and unfelt with you in your present "there," He nonetheless is there with you. How do we know? "For he hath said, I will never leave thee, nor forsake thee" (Hebrews 13:5).

"Beyond the fact that our God *cannot* lie, it is in fact *impossible* for Him to lie. The Lord God will never lie to us or mislead us. He will always tell us the truth, and fill us with truth from His Holy Word"[191] See Hebrews 6:18.

38 Consolation Gained through Song

"Let us sing even when we do not feel like it, for in this way we give wings to heavy feet and turn weariness into strength."[192]
~ John Henry Jowett

What do we do when something happens that doesn't make sense? We sing praises to God, as the psalmist David did. He said, "I will sing unto the LORD, because he hath dealt bountifully with me" (Psalm 13:6). To quote Spurgeon: "Any man can sing in the day—it is easy to sing when we can read the notes by daylight; but he is the skillful singer who can sing when there is not a ray of light by which to read."[193] Luther says, "This is a prayer [Psalm 13] full of the sighings and groanings of an afflicted heart in the hour of darkness, and almost overwhelmed under that darkness with the extreme of grief and sorrow and driven to the greatest strait of mind."[194] What brings on David's despondency (depression, downcast of soul, gloom)? The *feeling* that God had abandoned him and was disinterested in him and his trouble. He therefore prays, "How long wilt thou hide thy face from me?" (Psalm 13:1).

David's sadness is quickly replaced with song (Psalm 13:5–6). Spurgeon wrote, "The rain is over and gone, and the time of the singing of birds is come. The mercy-seat has so refreshed the poor weeper that he clears his throat for a song. As the shipwrecked mariner clings to the mast, so did David cling to his faith; he neither could nor would give up his confidence in the Lord his God. Oh, that we may profit by his example and hold by our faith as by our very life!"[195]

Whatever be our lot in life, knowing that God is with us in the midst of it spurs a song of praise, faith, hope, thanksgiving and heavenly anticipation. David's experience at this time doubtless led him later to say, "Yet the LORD will command his lovingkindness in the daytime, and in the night his song shall be with me, and my prayer unto the God of my life" (Psalm 42:8). As Paul and Silas were in jail following a brutal beating, it is said that they "prayed, and sang praises unto God" (Acts 16:25). God giveth His children a song to sing not only in the bright sunlight circumstances of life but in its midnights. Prayer and praises are divine medicines to mend the broken heart, lifting the soul from the pit of despair to the heights of delight. Through them Jesus will give "the oil of joy for mourning, the garment of praise for the spirit of heaviness" (Isaiah 61:3). G. J. Proctor said, "Little outwardly to cheer your life, very much to depress it. And yet you, too, may have songs of trust and loving confidence; songs of hope, and triumph in that hope."[196]

Sometimes a light surprises
    The Christian while he sings;
It is the Lord who rises
    With healing in his wings.
        ~ William Cowper (1731–1800)

Warren Wiersbe said, "If God doesn't see fit to remove our burdens, He always gives strength to bear them—and a song to sing while doing it!"[197]

39   *Oil of Joy for Mourning*

"No human heart, however wounded, continues always to bleed."[198]
~ Alexander Maclaren

What do we do when something happens that just doesn't make sense? We trust God to give us "beauty for ashes, the oil of joy for mourning, [and] the garment of praise for the spirit of heaviness [faint, feeble, weak; like a lamp that is about to go out[199]]" (Isaiah 61:3). The three-fold promise stated:

1. God will change our distraught countenance and disposition into its former radiance and beauty. Spurgeon states, "O mourning soul, thou hast made thine eyes red with weeping, and thy cheeks are marred with furrows, down which the scalding tears have burned their way; but the Lord that healeth thee, the Lord Almighty who wipeth all tears from human eyes, shall visit thee yet; and, if thou now believe in Jesus, He shall visit thee now and chase these cloudy griefs away, and thy face shall be bright and clear again, fair as the morning, and sparkling as the dew."[200]

2. He will grant consolation and comfort by the Holy Spirit. The Holy Spirit gives the mourner an anointing of the most exquisite "perfume" that produces unspeakable joy and peace. The plenteous tears that now configure the face and drench the soul will be wiped away by His consolation and comfort. He exchanges the tears of heaviness with the oil of joy. *Joy cometh in the morning* (Psalm 30:5). Barnes says, "There will be singing, shouting, exultation. That is, if we have the friendship of God, sorrow will always be temporary, and will always be followed by joy. The morning will come, a morning without clouds, a morning when the sources of sorrow will disappear."[201]

3. He will wrap us in heavenly praise that both expels the depressing and oppressing spirit and enables wondrous testimony of His magnificent goodness. Our despair will be turned into dancing, sorrow into singing and weariness into witnessing, which banishes the spirit of heaviness. This may only be wrought inwardly by the power of the Lord. It may not be manufactured or manipulated.

"Arise then, and sing, thou that sittest in the dust; put off thy sackcloth, and gird thee with gladness."[202] A good thing about having to drink from the cup of adversity is that it does have a bottom, an end.

40   *Hoping against Hope*

"Most men's faith is borne up by outward probabilities. They can trust God no further than they can see Him, but true faith dependeth upon Him when His way is in the dark."[203] ~ Thomas Manton

What do we do when something happens that just doesn't make sense? We hope against hope, against all "visible, rational grounds" of hope, as Abraham did (Romans 4:18).[204] Matthew Henry explains, "There was a hope against him, a natural hope. All the arguments of sense and reason and experience, which in such cases usually beget and support hope, were against him; no second causes smiled upon him, nor in the least favored his hope. But, against all those inducements to the contrary, he believed; for he had a hope for Him. He believed in hope, which arose, as his faith did, from the consideration of God's all-sufficiency."[205] Abraham did not stagger in unbelief, allow human rationale or logic to dampen his trust in God's promise (Romans 4:19).

When all natural hope is taken away, hope thou in God's promises. Paul did when upon a ship sailing for Rome, he encountered a hurricane. The storm was so fierce that he said, "All hope that we should be saved was then taken away" (Acts 27:20). Hoping against hope, Paul told the crew, "Be of good cheer: for there shall be no loss of any man's life among you, but of the ship" (Acts 27:22). He was able to manifest such hope (certainty, confidence) because he trusted the promise of God (Acts 27:23–24).

Don't bank your hope on the natural realm (upon that which is only logically possible and rational to expect), but upon supernatural God that specializes in miracles and who keeps all His promises (Luke 1:37 and Ezekiel 24:14a). Nothing is impossible when you put your trust in God, depending upon His Word.

"Difficulties must be thought on to quicken faith, not to weaken it. If they be pleaded against the promise, they weaken faith; if they be pleaded to drive us to the promise, they quicken faith."[206] Hold fast to God, hoping against hope, when that which is happening seems to be contrary to His promises to you.

41 Christ Is More Than Enough

"God sometimes brings us to the place where he brought Job to show us not only is God necessary, but God is enough."[207] ~ Adrian Rogers

What do we do when something happens that just doesn't make sense? We realize that despite the confusion and misunderstanding, Christ is sufficient to meet the need. With David, the believer says, "My flesh and my heart may fail, But God is the strength of my heart and my portion [sufficiency] forever" (Psalm 73:26, NASB). We desire or want none other than Christ. William Guthrie writes of Christ, "Less would not satisfy; more could not be desired."[208]Christ Himself is more than enough to enable us to cope with the trials, sorrows and hardships of life. Rest and reside in the knowledge that Christ Himself is all that you need. Christ says, "Don't worry—I am with you. Don't be afraid—I am your God. I will make you strong and help you. I will support you with my right hand that brings victory" (Isaiah 41:10 ERV). With Augustine, say, "Lord, give me Thyself."

The reason for rational hope and contentment in times of sickness or adversity is that Christ is the believers' portion of absolute sufficiency (Lamentations 3:24). "Christ is a rich Christ; He is a bottomless mine of merit and spirit, a boundless ocean of righteousness and strength, a full fountain of grace and comfort."[209] Rely upon Christ's omnipotent power, divine goodness and unchanging love to supply every need and sustain in the darkest of hours. If it be that the Lord is your portion, then depend upon Him to render the care, guidance, relief or help that is needed.

The soul that saith, "The Lord is my portion," is confident despite unsettling and disturbing news. The soul that saith, "The Lord is my portion," is calm despite the ferocious storm. The soul that saith, "The Lord is my portion," is comforted despite the piercing pain and grief. The soul that saith, "The Lord is my portion," is content despite the persecution, sickness or suffering. The soul that saith, "The Lord is my portion," is cheerful despite being distraught and anguished. The soul that saith, "The Lord is my portion," is courageous despite the great unknown. The soul that saith, "The Lord is my portion," is hopeful despite the dire hopelessness experienced (Habakkuk 3:17–18).

Other refuge have I none;
    Hangs my helpless soul on Thee.
Leave, oh, leave me not alone;
    Still support and comfort me.

All my trust on Thee is stayed;
    All my help from Thee I bring.
Cover my defenseless head
    With the shadow of Thy wing.

Thou, O Christ, art all I want;
    More than all in Thee I find.
Raise the fallen, cheer the faint,
    Heal the sick, and lead the blind.
        ~ Charles Wesley (1707–1788)

Adrian Rogers said, "You'll never know He is enough until He is all you have."[210]

42   No One Ever Cared for Me Like Jesus

"Man may dismiss compassion from his heart, but God never will."[211] ~ William Cowper

What do we do when something happens that just doesn't make sense? We remember that He is our sympathizing Father who is deeply concerned with the pain we bear. "When a tear is wept by you," saith Spurgeon, "think not your Father does not behold; for, 'Like as a father pities his children, so the Lord pities them that fear Him.' Your sigh is able to move the heart of Jehovah; your whisper can incline His ear unto you; your prayer can stay His hands; your faith can move His arm. Oh! think not that God sits on high in an eternal slumber, taking no account of you."[212] Octavius Winslow said, "Unlike changeable pity which sublimates into thin vapor—hollow, heartless, unsubstantial —Christ's sympathy, wakeful to every sigh of sorrow and spectacle of suffering, flows in streams of real and abiding blessing."[213]

Oh! then repeat the truth that never tires;
No God is like the God my soul desires.
He at whose voice Heaven trembles, even He,
Great as He is, knows how to stoop to me.[214]

Feelings matter to God. Every teardrop that flows from our eyes and grief borne deep in the soul is a concern to God. He sympathizes with us in our pain, for He is acquainted with our grief (Isaiah 53:3; Hebrews 4:14–16) and seeks to bind up our broken heart (Psalm 147:3). Henry Ward Beecher stated, "No physician ever weighed out medicine to his patients with half so much care and exactness as God weighs out to us every trial. Not one grain too much does He ever permit to be put in the scale."[215]

No one ever cared for me like Jesus;
There's no other friend so kind as He.
No one else could take the sin and darkness from me.
Oh, how much He cared for me!
~ Charles Weigle (1932)

D. L. Moody said, "Jesus will have compassion upon you. He will speak comforting words to you, not treat you coldly or spurn you. He is a faithful Friend—a friend that sticketh closer than a brother."[216] "I have cast my care on Thee, and I trust and am not afraid! To leave our times [Psalm 31:15] with God is to live as free from care as the birds upon the bough."[217]

43 Incredible Peace (Part One)

"If God be our God, He will give us peace in trouble. When there is a storm without, He will make peace within. The world can create trouble in peace, but God can create peace in trouble."[218] ~ Thomas Watson

What do we do when something happens that just doesn't make sense? We rely upon the peace of God for calm and assurance that all will be well. Paul says, "Then, because you belong to Christ Jesus, God will bless you with peace that no one can completely understand. And this peace will control the way you think and feel" (Philippians 4:7 CEV).

God's peace is provided through the Lord Jesus Christ (the Prince of Peace), and its foundation was rooted at Calvary (Romans 5:1; 8:1). Albert Barnes says, "Nothing else will furnish it but *Christ*. No confidence that a man can have in his own powers, no reliance which he can repose on his own plans or on the promises or fidelity of his fellow-men, and no calculations which he can make on the course of events can impart such peace to the soul as simple confidence in God."[219] "Only when our greatest love is God," writes Tim Keller, "a love that we cannot lose even in death, can we face all things with peace."[220]

It keeps ("guards") the heart free from fear (of the ungodly, misfortune, calamity, death, and Hell), doubt (it assures the believer that even amidst the worst of circumstances all is well, for God is their Protector and Guardian) and soul conflict and contention (anxiety, distress, worry).

Barnes states the peace of God keeps the saint "from murmuring at what God does, from petulance [cynicism] at what He does not. He can confide and wait, and believe and be thankful, suffer and be satisfied. The believer's peace is such as meets all the wants of the soul, silences the alarms of conscience, is fixed and sure amid all external changes, and will abide in the hour of death and forever."[221]

It's a peace so wonderful and marvelous that the ungodly dismiss it as mere foolishness (pipe dream, fantasy) and believers cannot articulate its height, depth, width or length, nor describe the fullness of the blessing it is (it "surpasses all understanding"—Philippians 4:7 NKJV). In what ways may the peace of Christ surpass the believers understanding (not experience)?

1. It instills a quietude and tranquilly when storms are confronted. They may shake and rattle the life but not thrust it into chaos or a disposition of sorrow and hopelessness like that which the ungodly experience in such times. Amidst the raging waters that batter the believer's ship, God gives a calm that is inexplicable.

2. It surpasses comprehension in the fact that it is manifest, regardless of whether or not the believer's prayer is granted.[222] To possess peace even when prayers for the healing of a loved one, a friend or ourselves are denied exceeds our intelligence to understand.

3. To sit in despair one moment, only to be lifted to a state of almost unbelievable serenity the next, brings mere amazement to the saint, but grave confusion to the unbeliever.

The world can neither give nor take,
Nor can they comprehend,
The peace of God which Christ has brought—
The peace which knows no end.
~ Selina, Countess of Huntingdon (1870)

44 Incredible Peace (Part Two)

"We have been given the peace of Jesus Christ. Even though I might not understand what's going on, I have a peace that bypasses my brain and permeates my heart. I might not know why things aren't working out, or why things are coming down, but in the midst of it all, Jesus offers me His peace."[223] ~ Jon Courson

To know the fullness of God's peace, keep your mind fixated upon Him. "Thou wilt keep him in perfect peace, whose mind is stayed on thee" (Isaiah 26:3). To know peace, acknowledge that the adversity, infirmity, or affliction experienced is purposed to bring you into closer conformity with God.[224] "God is chiseling you—you are but a rough block—He is making you into the image of Christ; and that sharp chisel is taking away much which prevents your being like him."[225]

In Philippians 4, Paul cites the formula to peace. To know peace, rejoice in the Lord (v. 4). To know peace, live in light of the coming (expectation) of Christ (v. 5). To know peace, relinquish anxieties to the Lord continuously through prayer (v. 6a). "Fret and worry indicate a lack of trust in God's wisdom, sovereignty, or power."[226] Wuest states, "The cure for worry is believing prayer."[227] To know peace, engage in thanksgiving for all things (v. 6c). John MacArthur states, "Inner calm or tranquility is promised to the believer who has a thankful attitude based on unwavering confidence that God is able and willing to do what is best for His children."[228] To know peace, protect what you think (v. 8). Give no place to wanton and disparaging thoughts. That is, give no place to fleshly impulses that trigger negative, unwholesome and unproductive thoughts. To know peace, let Paul's exemplary example in suffering and pain be the rule of conduct (v. 9). Imitate Paul's hope (Romans 12:12; 15:13), faith (2 Corinthians 12:9), focus (2 Corinthians 4:18) and mindset (Philippians 3:8).

God's peace is guaranteed. Wuest says, "The words *shall keep* are from a military word: 'shall mount guard.' God's peace, like a sentinel, mounts guard and patrols before the heart's door, keeping worry out."[229] "It is a pledge," Bradley says, "of the special love of God to the soul, and as such it begets confidence in Him. Let a worldly man lose his earthly comforts and he has lost all; but let a man of God lose what he may, his chief treasure is safe."[230] The world didn't give it (God's peace) to you, and the world can't take it away (John 14:27).

"The Christian is often surprised," saith Spurgeon, "at his own peacefulness. There is a possibility of having the surface of the mind lashed into storm, while yet, deep down, all is still. There are earthquakes, yet the earth pursues the even tenor of its way. It surpasses understanding, but not experience."[231] Know Christ; know peace—no Christ, no peace.

James McConkey writes, "For there is a peace which 'passeth all *mis*understanding'; a peace which keeps us, not we it; a peace of which it is said: 'Thou wilt keep him in perfect peace whose mind is stayed on thee'; a peace which, because born not of an outer calm, but an inner Christ, cannot be disturbed by sting or storm. How wondrous must be God's peace! And it is this peace that is ours to possess."[232]

45 Don't Depend upon Chariots and Horses

"Creature-confidence arms God against us and entails His curse on all who indulge it."[233] ~ Charles Simeon

What do we do when something happens that just doesn't make sense? We put our confidence in God, not in man and human resources. H. A. Ironside states, "How apt we are in the hour of stress and trial to turn for help to that which is merely earthly or human and so often fails us. If you once know the blessedness of depending on God, you will find it is a luxury to trust in Him. Your confidence will not be in the natural but in the spiritual."[234] Note: God may and often does use "horses and chariots" (doctors, medicine, therapists, friends) to accomplish His purpose in the believer who anchors His trust to Him foundationally and supremely. But the latter always determines the former.

To quote Spurgeon, "Chariots and horses make an imposing show and with their rattling and dust, and fine caparisons make so great a figure that vain man is much taken with them; yet the discerning eye of faith sees more in an invisible God than in all these."[235] However, instinctively some believers, instead of first looking to the Lord for help in the time of need, look to secondary sources and means (chariots and horses—Psalm 20:7). Like the unbeliever, they believe the more "chariots and horses" (human instrumentation instead of divine dependence) that are utilized, the greater the chance for deliverance, comfort, healing, or victory. Resolve not to be like them but to "let your faith be still more resolved to give up all dependence anywhere but upon God, and let your cry grow more and more vehement."[236]

But those looking to "chariots and horses" are wrong and partake of the bitter consequences of their error. "They [all that trust in 'chariots and horses'] are brought down and fallen [defeat and collapse]: but we [all that rely upon the Lord] are risen, and stand upright [successful, victorious]" (Psalm 20:8). "How different the end of those whose trusts are different"[237]! He that depends upon human ingenuity or ability or skill will be sorely disappointed and distressed, while the person that trusts in the Lord will be delighted and delivered. See Jeremiah 17:5–8. "It does not glorify God to trust Him when you have a thousand other props and assistances."[238]

In facing the giants of the unexplainable that bring pain and suffering, say to them each that which David said to Goliath: "You come to me using sword, spear, and javelin. But I come to you in the name of the Lord All-Powerful, the God of the armies of Israel" (1 Samuel 17:45 ERV). And you know how that turned out for Goliath!

46 *Don't Doubt in the Night What You Believed in the Light*

"Faith is the art of holding on to things your reason has once accepted, in spite of your changing moods."[239] ~ C. S. Lewis

What do we do when something happens that just doesn't make sense? We continue to trust God as we did when the sun was bright and sunny and everything made sense. Isaiah said, "Who among you fears the LORD and obeys his servant? If you are walking in darkness, without a ray of light, trust in the LORD and rely on your God" (Isaiah 50:10 NLT). With descriptive pen Isaiah describes the believer whose light has been extinguished for some unspecified reason (infirmity, affliction, bereavement, a "senseless or unfair" happening), whose hope is but all gone.

What is such a man to do? Isaiah counsels, "Let him *trust* in the name of the LORD, and *stay* upon his God." To trust in the "name of the LORD" is to rely upon, put confidence in and depend upon God to always do that which is for our eternal good. "The name of God, that is, God's attributes, and Christ's righteousness do sufficiently, and adequately, answer all wants and doubts, all objections and distresses."[240] It may be trusted to sustain in the dark as well as in the light. See Exodus 34:5–6.

What are we to do when the unexplainable happens? John Gill remarks, "Let him trust in the name of the Lord—not in himself, nor in any creature, but in the Lord Himself; in the perfections of His nature, His mercy, grace, and goodness; in the name of the Lord, which is a strong tower, and in whom is salvation; in Christ, in whom the name of the Lord is, and whose name is the Lord our Righteousness—and to trust in Him, when in the dark, is a glorious act of faith. This is believing in hope against hope. And stay upon his God; covenant interest continues in the darkest dispensation. God is the believer's God still; and faith is a staying or leaning upon Him, as such, a dependence upon His power to protect, on His wisdom to guide, and on His grace, goodness, and all sufficiency, to supply."[241] See Micah 7:8b and Psalm 20:7.

Don't doubt in the dark what God showed you in the light;
Truth won't go away if it's hidden from your sight.
God will never change, and His truth will remain.
So rest your heart; don't get lost in the dark.
Rest upon His faithful name.
~ Abigail Miller

Spurgeon said, "To trust God in the light is nothing, but to trust Him in the dark—that is faith."[242] An engineer of a train said, "The other night when I was on duty, there was a dense fog; we could not see a yard before us, but I knew that the permanent way was under us, and every now and then we caught a glimpse of some signal or other, and in time came safely to the journey's end." The Christian in times of deep darkness of soul must remember that the permanent way (track) is underneath him and all that he must do is maintain the course he was traveling prior to the onset of the deep darkness until the light returns. This is executed by faith in God and reliance upon His promises.

47   Questions Which Ought to Be Asked

"The great subject for wonder is, that while God has revealed Himself as the refuge of the oppressed, a friend in the day of calamity, a Savior from guilt, and sin, and hell, a comforter in darkness, and a deliverer in trouble, He should be neglected in circumstances and times when no other being and no other object can cheer the heart, or interpose any effectual relief."[243]
~ T. Kennion

What do we do when something happens that just doesn't make sense? We must be driven to ask the right questions with determination to get the right answers. "But many," Matthew Henry says, "that groan under great oppressions never mind God, nor take notice of His hand in their troubles. It should drive them to God, but how seldom is this the case!"[244] Elihu says, "But none saith, where is God my Maker, who giveth songs in the night; who teacheth us more than the beasts of the earth, and maketh us wiser than the fowls of heaven?" (Job 35:10–11).

In affliction, the question regarding God's presence, "Where is God my Maker?" ought to be asked foremost by the sinner. God is man's Maker and Sustainer, the omnipotent, omniscient and omnipresent Holy One of all creation (Deuteronomy 33:27; Psalm 46:1) and provider of eternal life. Where is He? The answer is somewhere and everywhere. He is within the seeker's eyesight and reach through the prayer of repentance and faith (Acts 20:21). Charles Simeon says, "To be satisfied with all that God does, and, in the absence of all human help, to trust simply and confidently in him, is an attainment far out of the reach of the natural man."[245] It's attainable only through a personal relationship with Jesus Christ.

The question regarding God's power, "Who giveth songs in the night?" ought to be asked by the sinner. It is necessary for it to be asked, for God alone has the compassion, love, authority and power to grant solace in sorrow, hope in despair and deliverance in trouble. Matthew Henry remarks, "He gives songs in the night; that is, when our condition is ever so dark and sad and melancholy, there is that in God, in His providence and promise, which is sufficient, not only to support us, but to fill us with joy and consolation and enable us in everything to give thanks, and even to rejoice in tribulation."[246] Spurgeon said, "Until divine grace comes in and changes our nature, there is none that saith, 'Where is God my Maker, who giveth songs in the night?'"[247]

The questions regarding God's provision, "Who makes us smarter than the animals of the earth and wiser than the birds of the air?" ought to be asked by the sinner. God has endued man with intellect, reasoning and wisdom above that of the animal world. *Beasts and fowls* have been given instincts regarding survival, shelter and acquisition of food, but none the ability to *know* God or look to Him for help. This capability was given to man alone. Regrettably, many men act as if they were on the level of the beasts of the field and fowl of the air when divine help is only a prayer away. See 1 John 5:20 and Jeremiah 31:33–34.

These questions and their answers reveal the absurdity and insanity of man to neglect God in affliction, infirmity and adversity. None can be a mighty refuge in the storm, comforter in the day of sorrow, forgiver of sin in failure, rescuer from Hell, and deliverer in the time of trouble other than the Lord. None other is worthy of trustfulness and so dependable to sustain in life's darkest and deepest trials. "Blessed is the man that trusteth in the LORD, and whose hope the LORD is" (Jeremiah 17:7). C. S. Lewis writes, "Faith in Christ Is the only thing to save you from despair."[248]

48 The Pillow on Which to Lay Your Head

"When you go through a trial, the sovereignty of God is the pillow upon which you lay your head."[249] ~ C. H. Spurgeon

What are we to do when something happens that just doesn't make sense? We remember that God's sovereignty enables Him to use the bizarre and senseless events of life for man's good, even when we can't fathom the how. "The lot is cast into the lap; but the whole disposing thereof is of the LORD" (Proverbs 16:33). Spurgeon well said, "If the simple casting of a lot is guided by Him, how much more the events of our entire life. It would bring a holy calm over your mind if you were always to remember this."[250]

John MacArthur states, "It's absolutely true that God is sovereign over every detail of our lives. No one acts apart from the sovereign plan of God. Every choice, every act, every decision made by every human in the world, including the most evil, heinous behavior against the truth and against the Lord, God overrules and fits into His plan for His own ends and His own glory."[251]

God's sovereignty means that He is unrestricted by time, space, or man's opposition to do whatever, whenever, however and with whomever what He chooses (Isaiah 46:10–11). He is self-existent (Psalm 90:2), limitless in power (Psalm 115:3), supreme in authority (Psalm 135:6), autonomous in rule (Deuteronomy 10:17), dependent upon nothing (Romans 11:36), all-sufficient (Job 22:2), the source and sustainer of all that exists (Hebrews 1:3; Isaiah 54:16), and the controller of the storms, winds, waves and tides (Matthew 8:26). What He speaks, happens (Isaiah 55:11).

He takes that which is meant by Satan to do evil (the senseless, bizarre, etc.) to His children to work for their best good (Romans 8:28; Genesis 50:20–21). He is the divine miracle worker that has power to supersede and overrule the work of nature and medical science when health declines (Psalm 77:14; Acts 19:11). He is the mighty counselor that grants wisdom to His children to know what to do and when to do it (Proverbs 3:32). He *alone* holds the keys of life and death (Job 14:5; Revelation 1:18; Hebrews 9:27).

Deane and Taswell state, "Events seem to be tossed about in the lap of chance. Yet just as surely as laws of motion govern the slightest movement of all the leaves that are blown by an autumn wind, Divine purposes control all human events, in the midst of their seeming confusion. This must be so if God is God."[252]

David Jeremiah said, "There are no accidents with God. So, wherever we find ourselves, and whatever we have to deal with, we can know that God, in His infinite wisdom and in His sovereignty, has designed it for our good and to make us like Christ and to bring Him glory. Just hang in there. You can trust God. He's in control and He's a good God."[253]

Sovereign Ruler of the skies,
Ever gracious, ever wise,
All our times are in Thy hand,
All events at Thy command.

Times of sickness, times of health,
Blighting wants and cheerful wealth,
All our pleasures, all our pains,
Come, and end, as God ordains.

May we always own Thy hand,
Still to Thee surrendered stand,
Know that Thou art God alone,
We and ours are all Thy own.
~ John Ryland (1777)

Arthur W. Pink stated, "To the one who delights in the sovereignty of God, the clouds not only have a 'silver lining,' but they are silver all through, the darkness only serving to offset the light!"[254] Saith Spurgeon, "The storm may rage, but all is well, for our Captain is the governor of storms. He who trod the waves of the Galilean Lake is at the helm, and at His command winds and waves are quiet" (Matthew 14:27).[255]

49   The Whispers of God

"The silvery tones of God's voice are constantly heard by those whose ears are inclined to hear."[256] ~ A. Clark

What are we to do when something happens that just doesn't make sense, prompting us to walk in a spiritual fog? We get to a quiet and calm place to hear the "gentle whisper" of God, like Elijah did (1 Kings 19:12). It's often in the seemingly senseless happenings of life that God speaks to us not through the "fire" or the "mighty wind," but rather, a "gentle whisper." And to hear those "whispers" requires solitude and sensitive spiritual hearing. See Psalm 62:1 and Matthew 11:25.

Open my ears that I may hear
Voices of truth Thou sendest clear;
And while the wave notes fall on my ear,
Everything false will disappear.
~ Clara H. Scott (1895)

What is this still small voice or whisper? It is Jesus speaking to our conscience through impressions by the Holy Spirit (Romans 8:14; John 15:4–5). These impressions or nudges at times serve as the believer's "fog lights" in difficult straits. They bring consolation, at times clarification of that which is being experienced, comfort and guidance. Therefore, it is expedient to learn to recognize it. The whispers of God will call us by our name, as was the case with Elijah and the child Samuel, making them personal. So, keep listening for Him to speak your name and then listen attentively and give heed.

Listen for the low whisper from the Throne
Speaking gently to you alone,
To comfort, strengthen, and cheer,
Reminding you that He's always near.
~ Frank Shivers (2021)

God may not answer our prayer through the fire or windstorm, causing us to think that He is silent or has deserted us. But 1 Kings 19:12 reminds us that often the means of His work lie not in public view, but in His divine whispers to our heart. "The most satisfactory proofs of the presence of God are found in the 'still small voice' with which he speaks to us."[257] "Speak, LORD, for thy servant is listening" (1 Samuel 3:7 NASB 1977).

50 Though He Slay Me

"Job said, in essence, "I trust God. No matter what happens, no matter what happens in my life, if He slays me, yet will I trust Him." That's the kind of faith it takes to get through the overwhelming world in which we live, to know that, first of all, we have a deep, unconditional connection with the God of the universe, and we trust Him. We trust Him."[258] ~ David Jeremiah

What do we do when something happens that just doesn't make sense, like what befell Job? We trust God. We strive to know Him better, to understand His heart and ways. We ever say with Paul, "That I may know Him" (Philippians 3:10). Job's loss, suffering and pain brought him to the conclusion that he might die. Therefore, he said, "Though he slay me [temporal death], yet will I trust in him" (Job 13:15). Included in the statement is not only *his* death, but all bereavements of friends and family members.[259] (If God took the most prized relationship from your heart, could you trust Him then?) He manifested hope (expectation, confidence) in God's control of his plight and walked in unwavering allegiance to Him. This was the case only because Job was a godly man that knew God intimately (Job 1:1).

"The better God is known," states Matthew Henry, "the more He is trusted. Those who know Him to be a God of infinite wisdom will trust Him further than they can see Him (Job 35:14); those who know Him to be a God of almighty power will trust Him when creature-confidences fail and they have nothing else to trust to (2 Chronicles 20:12); and those who know Him to be a God of infinite grace and goodness will trust Him though He slay them (Job 13:15). Those who know Him to be a God of inviolable truth and faithfulness will rejoice in His word of promise, and rest upon that. Those who know Him to be the everlasting Father will trust Him with their souls as their main care, and trust in Him at all times, even to the end."[260] To know God better theologically (Bible), experientially (fellowship with Him) and historically (His mighty works in the world and among man) strengthens faith in and dependence upon Him. Divine knowledge and intimate acquaintanceship take time to develop, so cultivate it unwaveringly (1 Peter 2:2; Luke 10:39).

51   Acquaint Thyself with Him

"Loving acquaintance with the revealed character of God lifts a man above earth and all its ills."[261] ~ Alexander Maclaren

What do we do when something happens that just doesn't make sense? "Acquaint now thyself with him, and be at peace: thereby good shall come unto thee" (Job 22:21). "Acquaint thyself with God."[262] Trust in God is based on acquaintanceship. Alexander Maclaren says, "Acquaintance with God is, not merely procures, good. To know Him; to clasp Him to our hearts as our Friend, our Infinite Lover, our Source of all peace and joy; to mold our wills to His and let Him dominate our whole selves; to seek our wellbeing in Him alone—what else or more can a soul need to be filled with all good? Acquaintance with God brings Him in all His sufficiency to inhabit else empty hearts. It changes the worst, according to the judgment of sense, into the best, transforming sorrow into loving discipline, interpreting its meaning, fitting us to bear it, and securing to us its blessings."[263] The most pertinent prayer the believer may pray is that of Paul: "I want to know Him. I want to have the same power in my life that raised Jesus from the dead. I want to understand and have a share in His sufferings and be like Christ in His death" (Philippians 3:10 NLV).

The man that genuinely and intimately knows God ("acquainted") says with Job, "Though He slay me, yet will I trust in him"—yet not without exertion. Faith and trust involve struggle and battle in specific trials. He must thwart the derision and temptations of others to get him to abandon the faith (Job 2:9). He must fight against the flesh that speaks contrary to his faith (Galatians 5:17). He must muster confidence in the person and promises of God equal to the challenge (Romans 10:17). He must believe God over personal perception (Luke 5:22; Isaiah 42:20). Ignorance of reasoning about what is happening will cry "distrust him." Weak faith will cry "distrust him." Medical science at times will cry "distrust him." Friends that surround you may cry "distrust him." Circumstances will cry "distrust him." But in knowledge of the character, conduct and compassion of God, say confidently, "I will trust him, though He slay me. Naked I came from my mother's womb, and naked shall I return there. The Lord gave, and the Lord has taken away; blessed be the name of the Lord" (Job 1:21).

52　A New Revelation of God

"One of the main ways we move from abstract knowledge about God to a personal encounter with him as a living reality is through the furnace of affliction."[264] ~ Timothy Keller

What do we do when something happens that just doesn't make sense and God doesn't apologize or explain Himself? We respond like Job, who never learned the reason for his suffering. Upon the ash heap where he suffered immense physical pain, through the harsh interrogations and accusations of the four friends and the honest dialogue with God, Job failed not to worship God and place that relationship utmost in his life above all others. Job came through the seemingly senseless experience with an elevated view of God, not a lower one (Job 42:5). Eric Ortlund states, "When we suffer without knowing why and persist in our relationship with God without any explanation or apology from Him, we too will have God stand before us as the Lord in a whole new way, as God in a way totally different from any other relationship we have."[265] "When you and I hurt deeply," Warren Wiersbe says, "what we really need is not an explanation from God but a revelation of God [His love, kindness, compassion, concern, mercy, care]."[266]

53 Stay in Tune with God

"Human fellowship can go to great lengths, but not all the way. Fellowship with God can go to all lengths."[267] ~ Oswald Chambers

What do we do when something happens that just doesn't make sense? We stay in tune with God through it all. Despite the abandonment of dearest friends, puzzlement over what happened, horrendous pain and sorrow and assailing doubts thrust in the soul by the enemy, stand immovable, unshakeable, always abounding in the faith and trustworthiness of God (1 Corinthians 15:58). Paul, in battling hardships, said, "Notwithstanding the Lord stood with me, and strengthened me" (2 Timothy 4:16–17).

And He will also strengthen us with peace, confidence and comfort not to break when tempted to break, to stand when tempted to stumble. Oswald Chambers says, "Allow nothing to keep you from looking with strong determination into the face of God regarding yourself and your doctrine [beliefs, convictions]. We must build our faith not on fading lights [friends, possessions, medical science] but on the Light that never fails."[268]

George Horne says, "Grounded on Him, by faith in His sufferings and exaltation, we may defy all the storms and tempests that can be raised against us by the adversary, while, as from the top of a lofty mountain on the shore, we behold the waves dashing themselves in pieces beneath us."[269] Spurgeon said, "Walk in your path of integrity with steadfast steps, and show that you are invincibly strong in the strength which confidence in God alone can confer. Thus, you will be delivered from anxious care, you will not be troubled with evil tidings, your heart will be fixed, trusting in the Lord."[270]

54   When You Can't Trace His Hand, Trust His Heart

"The Christian believes Him to be too wise to err and too good to be unkind; he trusts Him where he cannot trace Him, looks up to Him in the darkest hour, and believes that all is well."[271] ~ C. H. Spurgeon

What do we do when something happens that just doesn't make sense? Ultimately, "when you can't trace His hand, trust His heart." And His heart is full of compassion, love, kindness and tender mercy for us. The Bible says that we are so precious and special to God that He knows our name (Isaiah 43:1), that it is inscribed upon the palms of His hand (Isaiah 49:16), that never for a second are we out of His mind (Psalm 139:17–18), that He stores our tears in a bottle of remembrance (Psalm 56:8), that He is aware of our infirmities (Hebrews 4:15), and that He uses all that happens for our good (Romans 8:28).

God moves in a mysterious way,
    His wonders to perform.
He plants his footsteps in the sea
    And rides upon the storm.

His purposes will ripen fast,
    Unfolding ev'ry hour.
The bud may have a bitter taste,
    But sweet will be the flow'r.

Blind unbelief is sure to err
    And scan His work in vain.
God is His own interpreter,
    And He will make it plain.
        ~ William Cowper (1774)

Quoting Spurgeon again: "It is a poor faith which can trust God only when friends are true, the body full of health, and the business profitable; but that is true faith which holds by the Lord's faithfulness when friends are gone, when the body is sick, when spirits are depressed, and the light of our Father's countenance is hidden. A faith which can say in the direst trouble, 'Though he slays me, yet will I trust in him,' is Heaven-born faith."[272] Don't cater to "knee-jerk" reactions when God doesn't seem to make sense regarding infirmity, bereavement and adversity. Instead, steadfastly trust Him with what is happening, though the stars fall from the sky. "For we walk by faith, not by sight" (2 Corinthians 5:7).

Say not my soul, 'From whence can God relieve my care?'
Remember that Omnipotence has servants everywhere.
His method is sublime, His heart profoundly kind;
God never is before His time, and never is behind.
~ Thomas T. Lynch (1855)

55   The Best Is Yet to Come

"The life of a Christian is wondrously ruled in this world by the consideration and meditation of the life of another world."[273]
~ Richard Sibbes

What do we do when something happens that just doesn't make sense? We remember this life with its trials is not the final chapter of man's existence. The godly have a home even now prepared in Heaven (John 14:1–6) awaiting their arrival. Paul states, "But we are citizens of heaven, where the Lord Jesus Christ lives. And we are eagerly waiting for him to return as our Savior. He will take our weak mortal bodies and change them into glorious bodies like his own, using the same power with which he will bring everything under his control" (Philippians 3:20–21 NLT).

Samuel Rutherford said, "The hope of heaven under troubles is like the wind and sails to the soul."[274] Heaven is the believer's utopia, a place of reunion with Christ and loved ones in an eternal domain where "nothing will be sad, disappointing, deficient, or wrong."[275] Oh, how beautiful and wonderful Heaven must be!

"Too little do we, in the rivalries and anxieties of our human life, permit the blessed influences of that holy world to allure and to occupy us."[276] Scripture teaches that saints ought to think much about Heaven. Peter says, "But we are looking forward to the new heavens and new earth he has promised, a world filled with God's righteousness" (2 Peter 3:13 NLT). Paul wrote, "Set your affection on things above, not on things on the earth" (Colossians 3:2). Baxter says, "There is nothing else that is worth setting our hearts on."[277] In times of fierce conflict, pain, and trouble, remember the locality of your Home and that which awaits there.

56 That's What This Altar Is For

"Until I entered God's sanctuary. Then I understood." ~ Psalm 73:17 CSB

What do we do when something happens that just doesn't make sense? Outside of private worship we bear the inexplicable burden unto the Lord in His holy sanctuary. We don't abandon the church. "Worship puts our pain in its rightful place—under the reign of an already victorious Father."[278] Solace, comfort, joy and encouragement for the most horrendous pain and grief are found at Jesus' feet at the altar in the sanctuary. It was so for David in the anguish of soul he bore over the death of his baby boy (2 Samuel 12:20), and myriads of others before and since that brought their heavy burden to the Lord. The same experience awaits you (Psalm 24:5–6). When we worship Jesus, hearing from Him through the sermon, and singing His praises, He meets us with open arms of compassion, love, and tenderness to enable us to have coping strength and endurance. It is in the holy sanctuary that the Holy Spirit heals our broken heart and spirit. It is there where the saints of God minister to our hurt and shore us up in His strength and theirs alike. Jonathan strengthened David's grip on God (1 Samuel

23:16). Brothers and sisters in the household of faith await to do that for us, and also to spur us on with encouragement (Hebrews 10:24; 2 Corinthians 1:3–4; Galatians 6:2). "A burden shared is a lighter load."[279]

To summarize, Alexander Maclaren states that when we carry our grief into the sanctuary, there it immediately "changes its aspect and becomes a solemn joy."[280] Neglect not the sanctuary, for it is there relief and resolution are to be swiftly found (Psalm 63:1).

Ray Boltz wrote the song "That's What This Altar Is For," which depicts, in part, the altar's purpose: a place where despairing saints may bear their troubles and hardships to the Lord.

57 The Divine Comforter

"It takes great wisdom to comfort a broken heart. Only God can do it."[281] ~ C. H. Spurgeon

What do we do when something happens that just doesn't make sense? Rely upon the Holy Spirit to heal our broken heart and bear us up in the difficult trial. His office in the main is conviction of sin, yes, but also equally that of comfort. He is the believer's Comforter in trial and trouble (John 15:26). And none but He can render healing to the emotions that manifest devastating pain and misery which cause us to feel as if we have been torn open and are bleeding from every part of the body. Experience and observation attest that emotional wounds may be "clinically" resolved, only to remain hidden, unhealed for years, robbing us of joy and causing horrendous grief. To know complete healing takes a divine work of the third Person of the Holy Trinity. He is the antidote and cure for despondency, depression, grief, pain and agony of soul. J. C. Ryle said, "And *He* knows exactly how to comfort His afflicted people. He knows how to pour in oil and wine into the wounds of the spirit, how to fill up gaps in empty hearts, how to speak a word in season to the weary, how to heal the broken heart, how to make all our bed in sickness, how to draw nigh when we are faint, and say, 'Fear not: I am thy salvation' (Lamentations 3:57)."[282]

It is beyond amazing and glorious how the Holy Spirit carries and bears us up in times of agonizing loss, grievous sorrow, excruciating suffering and pain and especially in the inexplicable and insensible ordeals of life that shake life to its core (its waters and fires—Isaiah 43:2). It nearly surpasses human comprehension. See Psalm 34:17–20.

Pray. Dear Lord, hasten to my rescue. Consuming anguish is ravaging my life. I can't eat, sleep or have a moment's peace. I don't understand why this was allowed to happen, but do trust it in Your loving and gracious hands. My life is in constant turmoil and restlessness. I don't know what to do, which way to go. I feel all alone and am frightened at the unknown of tomorrow. I feel as if there is nothing but the darkness of dread and despair ahead. My hope is in You alone for help! Please send thy Holy Spirit to heal my broken heart and bind up my hurting wounds (Psalm 147:3). Come speedily and deliver me, I pray. In Jesus' name. Amen.

No storm can shake my inmost calm
　　　While to that Rock I'm clinging.
Since Love is lord of Heav'n and earth,
　　　How can I keep from singing?

What though my joys and comforts die?
　　　I know my Savior liveth.
What though the darkness gather round?
　　　Songs in the night he giveth.

The peace of Christ makes fresh my heart,
　　　A fountain ever springing!
All things are mine since I am His!
　　　How can I keep from singing?
　　　　　　~ Robert Lowry (1869)

58 One Step at a Time

"The man who measures things by the circumstances of the hour is filled with fear; the man who sees Jehovah enthroned and governing has no panic."[283] ~ G. Campbell Morgan

What do we do when something happens that just doesn't make sense? We look to our Shepherd to quiet our trembling heart, restore its peace and tranquility, and walk with us through the darksome valley each step of the journey. "Then he led out his people like sheep and guided them in the wilderness like a flock" (Psalm 78:52 ESV). Whatever the enormity of your "wilderness," the good Shepherd will guide you safely through it one step at a time to "green pastures" and "still waters" (Psalm 23:2).

The truth, was captured in an old country song by Marijohn Wilkin and Kris Kristofferson, "One Day at a Time, Sweet Jesus" (1974). L. B. Cowman writes, "This is the Blessed Life—not anxious to see far in front, nor careful about the next step, not eager to choose the path, nor weighted with the heavy responsibilities of the future, but quietly following behind the Shepherd, one step at a time."[284]

One step at a time, dear Savior;
    I cannot take any more.
The flesh is so weak and hopeless;
    I know not what is before.

One step at a time, dear Savior;
    I am not walking by sight.
Keep step with my soul, dear Savior;
    I walk by faith in Thy might.

One step at a time, dear Savior;
    Oh, guard my faltering feet!
Keep hold of my hand, dear Savior,
    Till I my journey complete.

One step at a time, dear Savior;
    Thou knowest all of my fear.
One word from Thy heart, dear Savior,
    And Heaven's mansions appear.
             ~ T. J. Shelton (1880)

59   To Spare from Future Evil

"We cannot be sure that a sudden and even (what we call) a premature death may not be a most merciful removal from intolerable pain, or from overwhelming temptation, or from grievous burdens and sorrows. We sing, 'Our times are in Thy hand,' and we do well to continue, 'O God, we wish them there.'"[285] ~ R. Clarkson

What do we do when something happens that just doesn't make sense, like the untimely death of a child, spouse, sibling or friend? We embrace Isaiah's theological perspective. Isaiah states saints die (at the time they do) to spare them from the evil days ahead (Isaiah 57:1–2). This was the case with Josiah (2 Kings 22:18–20). What a thought! Death is God's grace at work, protecting saints who die, from future heartache of immeasurable proportion (personal suffering, impending trouble, sore and grievous trial, a greater curse of evil in the world). Thus, death is a merciful friend! The bottom line—we die when God deems it best for us, perhaps for our family or others, and His glory. Earth's perspective fails to see Heaven's perspective (Isaiah 55:8–9) when death occurs. Our shortsightedness conceals what awaits down the road. In and by faith we now say with the psalmist what later will be substantiated a million times over: "Everything GOD does is right—the trademark on all his works is love. GOD'S there, listening for all who pray, for all who pray and mean it. He does what's best for those who fear him—hears them call out, and saves them. GOD sticks by all who love him, but it's all over for those who don't" (Psalm 145:17–20 MSG). Matthew Henry remarked, "The righteous are delivered from the sting of death, not from the stroke of it. They are taken away in compassion, that they may not see the evil, nor share in it, nor be tempted by it. The righteous man, when he dies, enters into peace and rest."[286]

J. R. Macduff writes, "Such early removals form a problem insoluble by our poor reason. They seem, at first sight, inconsistent alike with the Divine wisdom and power and love. They look almost like the frustration of God's plans and purposes, a failure in His sovereign designs. It is the architect just completing His work, when that work comes with a crash to the ground. It is the sculptor putting the finishing strokes of his chisel on the virgin marble, when the toil of months or years strews the floor of his studio. It is the gardener bringing forth from his conservatory the long-husbanded plants in their freshness and beauty, to bask in early summer sun, when a frost or hailstorm unexpectedly comes, and in one night they have perished!"[287]

60   Claim the Promises

"Every promise is built upon four pillars: God's justice or holiness, which will not suffer Him to deceive; His grace or goodness, which will not suffer Him to forget; His truth, which will not suffer Him to change; and His power, which makes Him able to accomplish."[288] ~ Salter

What do we do when something happens that just doesn't make sense? We claim God's promises as trustworthy and true (Joshua 21:45; 1 Kings 8:56) and apply them personally. "Whereby are given unto us exceeding great and precious promises: that by these ye might be partakers of the divine nature, having escaped the corruption that is in the world through lust" (2 Peter 1:4). Warren Wiersbe states, "God's people live by promises, not by explanations."[289] Spurgeon cautions, "We lose much consolation by the habit of reading His promises for the whole church, instead of taking them directly home to ourselves. Believer, grasp the divine word with a personal, appropriating faith. May the Holy Ghost make you feel them as spoken to you. Forget others for a while; accept the voice of Jesus as addressed to you, and say, "Jesus whispers consolation; I cannot refuse it. I will sit under His shadow with great delight."[290]

Use the promises. To quote Spurgeon again, "Do not treat God's promises as if they were curiosities for a museum, but believe them and use them."[291] Among the 7,147 promises[292] payable to the child of God, presently focus upon and appropriate personally several here and now. The promise of Isaiah 54:10 (NIV): "'Though the mountains be shaken and the hills be removed, yet my unfailing love [kindness] for you will not be shaken nor my covenant of peace be removed,' says the Lord, who has compassion on you"; the promise of Isaiah 41:10 (NIV): "So do not fear, for I am with you; do not be dismayed, for I am your God. I will strengthen you and help you; I will uphold you with my righteous right hand"; the promise of Romans 15:13 (NIV): "May the God of hope fill you with all joy and peace as you trust in him, so that you may overflow with hope by the power of the Holy Spirit"; the promise of Romans 8:38–39 (NIV): "For I am convinced that neither death nor life, neither angels nor demons, neither the present nor the future, nor any powers, neither height nor depth, nor anything else in all creation, will be able to separate us from the love of God that is in Christ Jesus our Lord."

What kept Paul from sinking down and going under in the face of multitudinous hardships and suffering? It was God's promises that he embraced personally (1 Timothy 1:12).

61   When There Is No Satisfactory Answer

"The question of 'Why?' has no satisfactory answer." [293] ~ John MacArthur

What do we do when something happens that just doesn't make sense? We don't add to the despair by looking for elusive answers for why it happened. In senseless tragedies there are no suitable or satisfactory answers. But answers aren't what we always need (even if they can be found), for they are impotent to provide innermost comfort or consolation. What is needed more than answers is faith in God's control and care in the circumstance and beyond it, and love from Him and others to survive it. John MacArthur's definition of faith, especially when applied to senseless happenings, is excellent. "Faith is simply breathing the breath that God's grace supplies."[294] Amen. And He will be faithful to provide new grace to cope with the devastating trial (John 1:16).

Grace is given on top of grace to enable coping, conquest and comfort. The grace that forgives sin is topped with new grace to move past the sin victoriously; grace given to relieve the broken heart is topped with new grace to start life anew amidst the pain; grace for hatred of sin gives way to grace to live a holy and blameless life; grace that copes with the storms of life is topped at life's end with new grace to die; grace bestowed to be a minister of the Gospel is topped with empowering grace to fulfill the task effectively; grace given to suffer the "thorns" of life without complaint is topped with grace to patiently bear the discomfort; the grace for close communion with Christ is topped with grace to conform more perfectly to His image; the grace to live in isolation or loneliness is topped with the sweetest of graces of having Christ as one's "all in all." Faith survives our crushed and broken spirits because it is infused with new grace. It satisfies the heart when there is no answer that does.

Matthew Henry beautifully expresses the believer's reaction to the senseless and bizarre happenings of life that have no explanation. "When we have so strong a faith in the Gospel of Christ as boldly to venture our souls upon it, knowing whom we have believed, then, and not till then we shall be willing to venture everything else for it."[295] That is, strong faith overrules feeling, fear, and perception, trusting God unquestionably with the unknown and unanswerable.

When answers aren't enough, there is Jesus.
He is more than just an answer to your prayer,
And your heart will find a safe and peaceful refuge.
When answers aren't enough, He is there.
~ Scott Wesley Brown

Dave Dravecky said, "I may not have the answers, but I do have Him."[296]

62   *The Lord Is Thy Keeper*

"Lord, I am going to expect Thee to do Thy utmost, and I am going to trust Thee day by day to keep me absolutely."[297] ~ Andrew Murray

What do we do when something happens that just doesn't make sense? We have the whole of God's omnipotence to help us each day cope with its pressures and pains. David knew the blessing of living beneath the canopy of divine omnipotence in the adversities and craziness of life. He counted God as His constant hiding place, tower of refuge, and deliverance; that he was kept in the hollow of God's hand; and that God took delight in him and sang over him. And in that sphere David lived. Too few believers live where he dwelt, to their own hurt.[298]

Allow the Almighty God to be thy Keeper of your affairs and cares (Psalm 121:5). Allow His omnipotence to maintain your cause (hope, comfort, consolation, strength) continuously (Psalm 140:12).

Andrew Murray said, "Will our God, in His tenderhearted love toward us, not keep us every moment when He has promised to do so? Oh! if we once got hold of the thought: Our whole religious life is to be God's doing—'It is God that worketh in us to will and to do of His good pleasure'—when once we get faith to expect that from God, God will do all for us. The keeping is to be continuous. Every morning God will meet you as you wake. If you trust the waking to God, God will meet you in the morning as you wake with His divine sunshine and love, and He will give you the consciousness that through the day you have got God to take charge of you continuously with His almighty power."[299] This He has promised and will do (1 Peter 1:5).

Moment by moment, I'm kept in His love;
Moment by moment, I've life from above.
Looking to Jesus till glory doth shine;
Moment by moment, O Lord, I am Thine!

Never a trial that He is not there,
Never a burden that He doth not bear,
Never a sorrow that He doth not share,
Moment by moment, I'm under His care.

Never a heartache and never a groan,
Never a teardrop and never a moan,
Never a danger but there on the throne,
Moment by moment He thinks of His own.

Never a weakness that He doth not feel,
Never a sickness that He cannot heal,
Moment by moment, in woe or in weal,
Jesus, my Savior, abides with me still.
~ Daniel W. Whittle (1840–1901)

"Are we wide enough awake to know that He is with us now? O blessed Savior, by Thy cross and passion, by Thy glorious resurrection and ascension, arouse all our spirits to perceive that Thou art not far from any one of Thy people, and that Thy word is still true: 'Lo, I am with you always, even unto the end of the world.'"[300]

63   Rest in What Jesus Said

What do we do when something happens that just doesn't make sense? Despite the many questions and unknowns involved, we surrender it wholeheartedly to the Lord. We rest it in the almightiness of God's hands, which is nothing but faith in action. Andrew Murray says, "In the beginning of the faith-life, faith is struggling; but as long as faith is struggling, faith has not attained its strength. But when faith in its struggling gets to the end of itself and just throws itself upon God and rests on Him, then comes joy and victory."[301]

A certain nobleman hoped that Christ might be able to heal his child, and therefore made the earnest entreaty. Christ's instant response to the man was, "Go thy way; thy son liveth" (John 4:50a). Without proof that his child in fact would live, he nonetheless chose to rest in the words of Christ (John 4:50b) and left for home believing what was told him. The story unfolds that as he neared his home in Capernaum, word came that his son had recovered at the exact time Jesus pronounced him whole (John 4:51–53). That father rested upon the words of Jesus that his son was healed (even without any evidence) and found it to be the case. That was faith in action.

The mysteries and unexplainables of life have no foundation upon which we may rest, outside of His promises to sustain. Like the nobleman, we must choose to say, "I have nothing on earth to trust in. I say to God, 'Thy word is enough; kept by the power of God.' That is faith; that is rest."[302] I will believe God over what my circumstances seem to say, and rest in Him to do that which is expedient in my behalf and that of others.

64   It May Get Darker Yet

"You may have to experience the very worst before you are delivered, but you will be delivered."[303] ~ F. B. Meyer

What do we do when something happens that just doesn't make sense and all the time appears to worsen? We trustingly, patiently wait on God's intervention, knowing though it be delayed (in the manner desired), it yet will come. Paul and Silas in a Philippian jail were not delivered until midnight (Acts 16:25–26). Peter, imprisoned by Herod for perhaps an Easter execution, miraculously escaped just before being summoned by the king (Acts 12:5–7). The four Hebrew children were not delivered until being thrust into the fiery furnace (Daniel 3:25). Joseph, imprisoned by the false accusations of Potiphar's wife, waited two years to be set free (Genesis 41:14). Jeremiah was pulled up by ropes from a giant pit (empty well) when it appeared he would die (Jeremiah 38:13). "It is always safe to trust God's methods and to live by His clock."[304]

Rescue at times happens quickly; other times it takes longer. Though your plight is worsening, don't faint. Maintain trust in God, who promises deliverance according to His plan and time. Wait upon the Lord a little longer and strength shall be renewed, life refreshed, and joy and peace restored (Isaiah 40:31). "Don't worry. God is always on time. Trust him."[305] He will come through for you. He will not fail you.

F. B. Meyer writes, "God may keep you waiting, but He will always remember His promise and will appear in time to fulfill His sacred Word that cannot be broken."[306]

65   Honor God in the Pain

"It glorifies God greatly for His servants to trust Him; they then become witnesses to His faithfulness, just as His works in creation are witnesses of His power and wisdom."[307] ~ C. H. Spurgeon

What do we do when something happens that just doesn't make sense? The great American pastor of the twentieth century, George W. Truett, admonished, "No matter what the trouble is, no matter what brought it, no matter who brought it, no matter how it came about, God is dishonored if a Christian does not bear his fiery trial like he ought to bear it. You will either dishonor Him egregiously, or you will honor Him gloriously, according to your behavior when trouble is on. Trouble rightly borne will surely honor God. Remember that."[308]

In the inexplicable happenings of life, though smote with indescribable grief, pain, doubt and panic, bear it as a good soldier of the Lord Jesus Christ, giving reason for the faith that is within you. "When you are living by faith," writes Alan Redpath, "through the darkness of circumstances, other people become aware of the radiance and sweetness of your life, and they are truly blessed."[309] And the opposite also is true.

66 Eleventh-Hour Miracles

"Beyond the clear statements of the biblical text, one would have to admit that miracles happen in present-day life. I believe God does heal today—sovereignly, supernaturally, radically and dramatically."[310] ~ Adrian Rogers

What do we do when something happens that just doesn't make sense and it appears God will not intervene? We remain calm and trustful that God is at work in ways we know not to fulfill His purpose with what happened and that in His time a miracle will be witnessed (unless He reveals otherwise). "The things which are impossible with men are possible with God" (Luke 18:27).

Eleventh-hour miracles happen all the time. Recall, it wasn't until Daniel was thrust into the den of lions that God intervened, binding shut the lions' mouths (Daniel 6:22). This he was not told would happen. Sometimes, for reasons known unto God, we walk the plank of trial and grave suffering, not knowing whether or not deliverance will come until the last moment, as was the case with Daniel.

(Note that although Scripture is silent about Daniel's faith in this dark hour, it mentions the strong faith of the king,

Daniel 6:16, 20). Thankfully, when our faith is weak in trial, God sends another to shore it up. Martin Luther received the solemn news of the approaching death of his bosom friend, Philip Melanchthon. Immediately he set out on the 150-mile journey to visit his friend and pray for his recovery. Luther found his friend at death's door and content to die. Relentlessly, he prayed for his friend and pressed upon him the need to eat. Melancthon finally ate the food prepared, immediately improved, and was speedily restored to health. For years afterwards was used mightily for God's cause. Luther, in recounting the miracle to his wife, Catherine, said, "God gave me my brother Melanchthon back in direct answer to prayer."[311] Eleventh-hour miracles happen!

"It is impossible to believe in a sovereign God and not believe in miracles."[312]

67   A Peace Which Keeps Us

"A peace which keeps us, not we it."[313] ~ James McConkey

What do we do when something happens that just doesn't make sense? We rest in the peace of God that keeps us safe and secure (not we it). Why or how? McConkey answers, "A peace which, because born not of an outer calm, but an inner Christ, cannot be disturbed by sting or storm. It is the peace of the fullness of the Spirit."[314]

> Human, man-made peace, which rises and falls with the vicissitudes of life, is worthless; but the peace of CHRIST, what a gift is this!
> James McConkey

Meditate a moment upon the vastness and richness of God's peace that is able to keep you sane, rational and stable in the worst of storms that batter against your life. "How wondrous must be GOD'S peace! With Him there is no frailty, no error, no sin. With Him there is no past to lament; no future to dread; no blunders, no mistakes to fear; no plans to be thwarted; no purposes to be unmet. No death can overcome, no suffering weaken, no ideal be unfulfilled, no perfection unattained. Past, present or future; vanishing time or endless eternity; life or death; hope or fear; storm or calm—naught of these, and naught else within the bounds of the universe, can disturb the peace of Him who calls himself the GOD OF PEACE. And it is this peace that is ours to possess. 'THE PEACE OF GOD shall keep YOUR heart and minds' (Philippians 4:7). Not a human peace attained by self-struggle or self-discipline, but Divine peace—the very peace which God himself has, yea, is. This is why Jesus Himself says, 'My peace I give unto you.' Human, man-made peace, which rises and falls with the vicissitudes of life, is worthless; but the peace of CHRIST, what a gift is this!"[315]

"My peace." It is a promised peace that shields the believer from the utter devastation and maniac depression that the bizarre and inexplicable happenings of life bring. It is a promised peace that works its task whether or not prayers are answered according to our desire. It is a promised peace that will kick in immediately upon request, despite chaos of heart, life and circumstances. "Don't worry over anything whatever; tell God every detail of your needs in earnest and thankful prayer, and the peace of God which transcends human understanding, will keep constant guard over your hearts and minds as they rest in Christ Jesus" (Philippians 4:6 PHILLIPS).

68   The Darkest Hour

"Despondency sets all his songs to a minor key. It gives to all his prayers a wailing pathos. It takes away much of his buoyancy and elasticity for work."[316] ~ W. M. Taylor

What do we do when something happens that just doesn't make sense and we are experiencing the darkest hour of despondency? The despondency may have resulted from a death, disease, or disaster. But it has baffled and paralyzed the heart. What are we to do when the night is so dark that we can't even see a ray of light? As has been stated repeatedly in this book, we exhibit faith in God and trust Him explicitly. Don't allow the darkness to dictate your peace, joy, hope or future. Let that be determined by reliance upon the Lord. In the depth of darkness, we focus on the coming light promised. "Weeping may endure for a night, but joy cometh in the morning" (Psalm 30:5).

Granted, the night lasts a lot longer than anticipated (months, years, and for some a lifetime). But a time will arrive when the night gives way to rejuvenation about life. The wondrous thing about the darkest and longest of nights is that they always end. William Cowper wrote, "The darkest day, if you live till tomorrow, will have passed away."[317]

Each moment spent within its tunnel, you are ever moving, though at times at a snail's pace, toward the light Christ promised when the birds would be heard chirping and the sun would be seen shining again. Until that happens, Christ holds us in His loving, everlasting arms of consolation, comfort and peace. He makes sure that we will come out on the other side of the darkness, equal to meet its challenges, with renewed hope and restored joy. Don't drown in despair. The darkness will be enveloped in His Light.

Tis better to walk by faith than sight
    In this path of yours and mine;
And the pitch-black night, when there's no outer light,
    Is the time for faith to shine.[318]
            ~ Unknown

69   The Lifting of the Sorrow

"Perhaps you don't want to survive in your present anguish, but as the hours and the days go by, our minds and bodies adapt to whatever is the cause of our grief, and slowly we do realize that we are surviving. We shall never forget, but we shall cope."[319] ~ C. S. Lewis

What do we do when something happens that just doesn't make sense and we want to give up? We respond similarly to the crushing happening, as C. S. Lewis did. Upon the death of C. S. Lewis' wife, Helen Joy (married only three years), he profoundly lamented. "And grief still feels like fear; perhaps, more strictly, like suspense; or like waiting—just hanging about waiting for something to happen. It gives life a permanently provisional feeling. It doesn't seem worth starting anything. I can't settle down. I yawn; I fidget; I smoke too much. Up till this I always had too little time. Now there is nothing but time, almost pure time, empty successiveness. One flesh, or, if you prefer, one ship—the starboard engine has gone. I, the port engine, must chug along somehow till we make harbor, or rather, till the journey ends. How can I assume a harbor?"[320]

Lewis's description of grief over the death of Helen crushes our heart, but such is the agony of all who lose a loving and honorable life's mate. Sometimes we don't empathize with widows or widowers deeply enough. It's not that we will understand. That will never happen. After all, it was their treasured loved ones who died, not ours. But we can strive to understand why they lament so deeply and excessively (according to our thinking) for so long and at times in such strange and unique ways. Our sympathy and empathy will enhance removal of the sorrow as we exercise patience with their grief.

Following several weeks of being distraught, Lewis states that something unexpected and unusual happened. It happened that "the sun was shining and there was a light breeze. And suddenly, at that very moment, I mourned Helen least; I remembered her best. It was something (almost) better than memory—an instantaneous, unanswerable impression."[321] Lewis said that to say the experience was like seeing her would be over the top, yet he was prone to use such words. And that experience for him lifted the barrier of sorrow.[322] His assessment: "You can't see anything properly while your eyes are blurred with tears [or when overcome with exhaustion]."[323] "You will weep and mourn while the world rejoices. You will grieve, but your grief will turn to joy" (John 16:20 NIV).

As it was with Lewis, the barrier that prevented joy over sorrow will be lifted, perhaps when least expected. But it will happen as you trust God. Today may be that day.

70   *There Is More beyond Death*

"When I go down to the grave, I can say, like so many others: I have finished my work, but I cannot say I have finished my life. My day's work will begin the next morning. My tomb is not a blind alley. It is a thoroughfare. It closes in the twilight to open in the dawn."[324] ~ Victor Hugo

What do we do when something happens that just doesn't make sense and takes a beloved friend or family member suddenly to Heaven? We place it at the altar in the stack of the unexplainables that one day will be clarified, and look with joy toward the glorious reunion with our friend that died in the Lord. We focus on the known, not the unknown.

We will see and know them in Heaven. On the Mount of Transfiguration, Moses and Elijah, in their heavenly (resurrected) bodies, were recognized by the disciples (Matthew 17:1–4). Mary recognized Jesus in His resurrected body (John 20:16). Jesus said that saints will see "Abraham, and Isaac, and Jacob, and all the prophets, in the kingdom of God" (Luke 13:28), clearly meaning they will be recognizable. A rich man (Dives) sorely treated a beggar named Lazarus at his gate. Upon death, Lazarus was escorted by the angels to Heaven, while the rich man was cast into outer darkness in Hell. From the chambers of Hell, the man recognized Lazarus in Heaven (Luke 16:23). To Mary, the distraught, grieving sister of Lazarus (a different Lazarus than he in Luke 16), Jesus said, "Thy *brother* shall rise again" (John 11:23). In death, he yet was her brother; and she, his sister.

"The tomb is not a blind alley. It is a thoroughfare. It closes on the twilight. It opens on dawn."[325] Let this excite hope and expectancy and consolation. You will meet your loved one again. And at most, that will not be long.

There will be a happy meeting in Heaven I know,
When we see the many loved ones we've known here below
Gather on the blessed hilltops with hearts all aglow;
That will be a glad reunion day.
~ Adger M. Pace (1940)

71   *The Cross Is the Crux of It All*

"In order for the human heart to maintain love for a sovereign God, faith must affirm what it cannot prove. We must believe that God has a good purpose for the awful things that occur to us."[326]
~ Bryan Chapell

What do we do when something happens that just doesn't make sense? We respond the way a miner did, a devout Christian who became an invalid at an early age due to an injury. Over the years, through his window, he saw friends and fellow workers marry, raise families, and have grandchildren. Through his window, he witnessed the company he once served expanding and thriving without reaching out to assist him adequately. Day by day he watched these things and many others as his body withered, his house crumbled and his hope for things to change died.

The day came when the aged miner became bedridden. A young man visited him, saying, "I hear that you believe in God and claim that He loves you. How can you believe such things after all that has happened to you?" The old man smiled and said in response, "Yes, there are days of doubt. Sometimes Satan comes calling on me in this fallen-down old house of mine. He sits right there by my bed, where you are sitting now. He points out my window to the men I once worked with whose bodies are still strong, and Satan asks, "Does Jesus love you?" Then Satan makes me look at my tattered room as he points to the fine homes of my friends and asks again, "Does Jesus love you?" Finally, Satan points to the grandchild of a friend of mine—a man who has everything I do not—and Satan waits for the tear in my eye before he whispers in my ear, "Does Jesus really love you?"

The visitor inquired, "And what do you say when Satan speaks to you in that way?" The miner replied, "I take Satan by the hand, and I lead him to a hill far away called Calvary. There I point to the nail-scarred hands, the thorn-torn brow, and the spear-pierced side. Then I say to Satan, 'Doesn't Jesus love me?'"[327]

A firm theology of the Cross makes the inexplicable happenings of life bearable and consolable. To say in utter confidence and faith in the wake of the cruelest of circumstances, "Jesus loves me," is the believer's refuge and strong tower to weather victoriously the pain, hurt, suffering and sorrow the way the miner did. Jerry Bridges said, "If we want proof of God's love for us, then we must look first at the Cross where God offered up His Son as a sacrifice for our sins. Calvary is the one objective, absolute, irrefutable proof of God's love for us."[328] All that happens to the Christian must be viewed against the backdrop of Calvary. That's the crux of man's hope and peace despite what shakes and crushes our world.

72 Don't Let It Drown out the Music

"When you are not walking with the Lord, you lose your song and start living on memories."[329] ~ Warren Wiersbe

What do we do when something happens that just doesn't make sense and seeks to extinguish our life's song? We refuse to allow the inexplicable happening to mar or spoil the music that Christ birthed into our soul at conversion. Though our face has wet cheeks, our heads hang down in gloom, and our spirit is melancholy, we must keep singing His song, for it's the Christian's hope, consolation, and peace. Gloom may suppress it but must never sequester it.

Without Christ's song alive, we gradually die. It's His song that gives continued meaning, purpose and happiness to life when we are smitten with an incurable disease, devastated with trouble, or have the love of our life snatched away. "For you have been my help, and in the shadow of your wings I will sing for joy" (Psalm 63:7 ESV).

Ye saints, who toil below, adore your heavenly King,
And onward as ye go, some joyful anthem sing.
Take what He gives and praise Him still
Through good and ill who ever lives.
                    ~ Richard Baxter

73   *"There's a Hole in the World Now"*

"Death leaves a heartache no one can heal; love leaves a memory no one can steal." ~ Irish headstone

What do we do when something happens that just doesn't make sense? With God's help, you cope and heal and await the day when you will be reunited with your departed loved one. Upon the death of his twenty-five-year-old son in a mountain climbing accident, Nicholas Wolterstorff wrote the book *Lament for a Son,* in which he states, "There is a hole in the world now."

That's how we all feel when death takes a loved one from our life. There is a huge hole that nothing can fill. Friends and family try to fill it. We even try to fill it ourselves in time. But the effort is futile. The hole remains. The death of a loved one is like an amputation of an arm or a leg which you will live without for the rest of your life. (Life is lived with unmitigated pain and wistfulness and continual remembrance.) "Sorrow is not a stage you get through, but rather a process you live with" by the grace of God.

How did the theologian Wolterstorff handle the untimely death of his son? His search for a comfort that neatly could be packaged for himself and his family was futile.[330] Instead, he found this: "It is a great mystery. To redeem our brokenness and lovelessness, the God who suffers with us did not strike some mighty blow of power but sent His beloved Son to suffer like us, through His suffering to redeem us from suffering and evil. Instead of explaining our suffering, God shares it."[331]

God's Son, Jesus, knew suffering almost from the start upon His arrival to earth. The prophet Isaiah prophesied three hundred years prior to His arrival that which literally would transpire: "He is despised and rejected of men; a man of sorrows, and acquainted with grief" (Isaiah 53:3). And at the young age of 33 He was hung on a Cross to suffer and die for man's sin in full view of His mother on earth and Father in Heaven. On Easter morning, three days later, Jesus was raised from the dead, fulfilling the promise that Paradise lost would be Paradise regained (a day is forthcoming when God's perfect design of creation will be restored on earth).

Jesus' suffering, death and resurrection also opened the door to Utopia, that of Heaven where they that die knowing Him will forever live with Him. This Home of the saved knows no tears, sorrows, sufferings or sad goodbyes. It is here where that "hole in your world" will finally be filled by the reunion with him whose absence created it. Hallelujah and amen!

74 Don't Sleep through the Blessing

"Let us not sleep, as do others"; for there are many who are so soundly sleeping that they are quite oblivious of the glories of Christ."[332] ~ C. H. Spurgeon

What do you do when something happens that just doesn't make sense? You devote yourself to the reading and absorption of the Word of God during the long nights when sleep is elusive. You say with the psalmist, "I rise before the dawning of the morning, And cry for help; I hope in Your word. My eyes are awake through the night watches, That I may meditate on Your word" (Psalm 119:147–148 NKJV). Although sleep is vitally important to health, the Word of God provides rich medicine to heal the soul. "He sent his word, and healed them, and delivered them from their destructions" (Psalm 107:20).

Early in the pre-dawn, Jesus was praying and meditating on the Scripture on the Mount of Transfiguration, He, Moses and Elijah discussed His impending death. All the while, Peter, James, and John slept (Luke 9:32). They slept through the blessing. We probably do the same more than we realize by being insensitive to the Spirit's nudge to awaken to meet with the Lord, or by thoughtlessness to do so when we are awake. Many a hurting saint has found Psalm 107:20 to be true while praying and meditating upon the promises in the night. "He sent His word and healed me, and delivered me from my troubles" (my paraphrase).

David coupled crying out to God for help (prayer) with meditation upon His Word. The two go together. Often the Lord uses the Word to respond to the cry of our heart. That's why it's essential to keep a Bible on your nightstand for easy access during the night hours. In this your time of deepest hurt and puzzlement over what has happened, don't discount the healing medicine that awaits in the quiet night hours when the world is at sleep. Don't be like the disciples and sleep through the blessing God has in store for you.

75   The Double Sinking

"True faith is keeping your eyes on God when the world around you is falling apart." ~ Unknown

What do you do when something happens that just doesn't make sense? Spurgeon comments, "Soul and body are so intimately united that one cannot decline without the other feeling it. We, in these days, are not strangers to the double sinking which David describes; we have been faint with physical suffering and distracted with mental distress."[333] What are we to do? That which David did. He said, "But I trusted in thee, O LORD: I said Thou art my God" (Psalm 31:14). "This man's eyes took in all surrounding evils, and these drove him to avert his gaze from them and fix it on Jehovah. That is the best thing that troubles can do for us. If they, on the contrary, monopolize our sight, they turn our hearts to stone; but if we can wrench our stare from them, they clear our vision to see our Helper."[334] When overwhelmed by affliction, infirmity or adversity, focus your gaze on the Lord, not on your circumstance, and He will cause you to rejoice. "Unto thee, O LORD, do I lift up my soul" (Psalm 25:1). "Mine eyes are ever toward the LORD; for he shall pluck my feet out of the net" (v. 15). "Because he has focused his love on me, I will deliver him. I will protect him because he knows my name. When he calls out to me, I will answer him. I will be with him in his distress. I will deliver him, and I will honor him" (Psalm 91:14–15 ISV).

John MacArthur said, "The more you focus on yourself, the more distracted you will be from the proper path. The more you know Him and commune with Him, the more the Spirit will make you like Him. The more you are like Him, the better you will understand His utter sufficiency for all of life's difficulties. And that is the only way to know real satisfaction."[335] Keep your focus not upon your trials and adversities or family, finances, future, or even ministry, but upon the Lord.

76 *Faith Doesn't Always Make Sense*

"To one who has faith, no explanation is necessary. To one without faith, no explanation is possible." ~ Thomas Aquinas

What do you do when something happens that just doesn't make sense? We exhibit faith, even when it doesn't make sense. Noah's step of faith to build the ark in a desert place in a time when rain *perhaps* (Hebrews 11:7) had never occurred seemed senseless (Genesis 6:14), but it produced a means of survival. Faith didn't make sense to Naaman, stricken with leprosy, to wash himself in the muddy Jordan River for healing (2 Kings 5:13–14), but it brought about a healing. David's faith in confronting Goliath didn't make sense, but it conquered the giant (1 Samuel 17:37). The faith of Shadrach, Meshach, and Abednego regarding the fiery furnace didn't make sense, but it granted deliverance (Daniel 3:26–27). These examples along with millions of others prove that faith works in the worst and most challenging of times, even when it seems futile, inadequate, impotent, and senseless to exhibit. It has an indisputable track record.

Let it do its work, even if at first with doubting and disputation. "Lord, I believe; help thou mine unbelief" (Mark 9:24). It alone makes the senseless and bizarre happenings of life *more* acceptable and bearable. It spurs hope, peace and mental well-being. Faith says that although what happened has no satisfying answer, God will work good from it and in His time reveal its purposes. Adrian Rogers said, "Faith sees the invisible, believes the incredible, knows the unknowable, and receives the impossible!"[336] With that kind of faith, God enables us to survive the worst of life's troubles and sorrows and maintain confidence in His divine providential control. Though faith may be as small as a mustard seed (the smallest seed known, according to the Parable of the Mustard Seed, measuring roughly 0.1 by 0.03 millimeters), it is sufficient to command mountains of problems, troubles and sorrows away, if it is rested upon the unchanging promises and words of Christ (Matthew 17:20).

77   A Fixed Heart Grants Calm

"God is fixed, and it is a simple truth that man is never fixed until he is fixed upon God. Surely a house, as to its fixedness, depends upon the foundation. Build a house on the sand, and is it fixed? You may fix it there as you think, but is it fixed? The foundation shifts, and what becomes of the house? Oh! the heart can only be fixed according to the fixedness of that on which it rests."[337] ~ Capel Molyneux

What do we do when something happens that just doesn't make sense? We dig our feet in the sod and say, "Although I don't understand why God allowed this to happen, I shall not be moved one iota from my belief and trust in God." With the psalmist, we say, "My heart is fixed, O God, my heart is fixed: I will sing and give praise" (Psalm 57:7).

The man whose heart is "fixed, trusting the Lord" has confidence that nothing can touch him that does not first pass through the hands of God. He knows that even in the darkest of days he stands beneath the umbrella of God's unfailing love and care. "There is no fear in love; but perfect love casteth out fear: because fear hath torment. He that feareth is not made perfect in love" (1 John 4:18).

Spurgeon stated, "Christian, you ought not to dread the arrival of evil tidings; because if you are distressed by them, what do you more than other men? Other men have not your God to fly to; they have never proved His faithfulness as you have done, and it is no wonder if they are bowed down with alarm and cowed with fear. But you profess to be of another spirit; you have been begotten again unto a lively hope, and your heart lives in Heaven and not on earthly things. Now, if you are seen to be distracted as other men, what is the value of that grace which you profess to have received? Where is the dignity of that new nature which you claim to possess?"[338]

A fixed heart is the negation of panic, fear and cowardice. He that possesses a fixed heart is constantly sustained by the sovereign hand of Almighty God. Lockyer says, "He is no rolling stone, but firmly settled by experience, and confirmed by years. Consequently, along with his holy heart, he has a brave face. He has no fear what men or demons may do"[339]—or what evil he may have to experience.

78   Going through the Confusion

"There are storms that will try the firmest anchors."[340] ~ Matthew Henry

What do we do when something happens that just doesn't make sense, causing us to almost stumble? In the straits of extreme difficulty and trial, especially when it is inexplicable, what believer hasn't said at some time, "My feet were almost gone; my steps had well nigh slipped" (Psalm 73:2)? The complicated mysteries of Divine providence at times challenge our faith, heaving hard on its anchors. A believer's long-held theology may be shattered or at least weakened severely due to a calamity that doesn't "fit" those embraced beliefs. James Dobson says, "Interestingly enough, pain and suffering do not cause the greatest damage. Confusion is the factor that shreds one's faith."[341] That is, the problem isn't with the pain but with puzzlement and bafflement with that which happened and why God allowed it to happen. "Jesus said that there are times when your Father will appear as if He were an unnatural Father—as if He were callous and indifferent—but remember, He is not."[342]

What is the Christian to do in such times of theological confusion? He must lean upon the fact that God never said in the Word that all would be understandable or explainable to our finite minds, but all would be founded in love and with our best good in mind. The Christian must understand that the determination to persevere when proof is absent and questions aren't answered is the very heart of the Christian faith.[343] J. Haldane Stewart said, "The way by which Christ leads His people is that of simple confidence in Him. He directs them not to judge Him by the outward appearances of His providence at a dark and unfavorable moment, but by His sure word of promise (Isa. 50:10)."[344]

Oswald Chambers said, "There are times in your spiritual life when there is confusion, and the way out of it is not simply to say that you should not be confused. It is not a matter of right and wrong, but a matter of God taking you through a way that you temporarily do not understand. And it is only by going through the spiritual confusion that you will come to the understanding of what God wants for you."[345] Chambers continues, "'When the Son of Man comes, will He really find faith on the earth?' (Luke 18:8). Will He find the kind of faith that counts on Him in spite of the confusion? Stand firm in faith, believing that what Jesus said is true, although in the meantime you do not understand what God is doing. He has bigger issues at stake than the particular things you are asking of Him right now."[346]

79 The Terrifying Night of Fright

"In every step of our way to Zion, we must cry, 'Hold Thou me up, and I shall be safe.'"[347] ~ Charles Simeon

What do we do when something happens that just doesn't make sense and terrifies us? We endeavor to listen to and obey the Lord, who said, "Thou shalt not be afraid for the terror by night" (Psalm 91:5). The statement itself reveals that "terror by night" (adversity, infirmity, unseemly deaths) happens at unexpected times ("night"), and when it occurs, the believer is to remain serene and safe by sheltering beneath the wings which overshadow him. "He that dwelleth in the secret place of the most High shall abide under the shadow of the Almighty" (Psalm 91:1). Panic- and horror-filled nights of terror are for the ungodly, not him that has proven God over and over again as just, holy, loving and kind in all that He does or allows.

Spurgeon states, "Remember that the voice which saith 'thou shalt not fear' is that of God himself, who hereby pledges His word for the safety of those who abide under His shadow—nay, not for their safety only, but for their serenity."[348] See Titus 1:2. The Bible says, "For God hath not given us the spirit of fear; but of power, and of love, and of a sound mind" (2 Timothy 1:7).

80 Yet in Heaviness, You Will Survive

"We don't root our happiness in circumstances, because those can change in an instant and leave us emotionally stranded. We root our joy in Christ alone, who is the same yesterday, today, and forever."[349] ~ Adrian Rogers

What do we do when something happens that just doesn't make sense? The Bible does not say that the believer will not be tempted or be in "heaviness" through manifold temptations (trials, troubles, tribulations), but that ultimately he will overcome them (1 Peter 1:6–7). Peter had his times of "little faith" (Matthew 14:31), as did Paul (Acts 18:9–10) and John the Baptist (Matthew 11:3) in trials. But they came out on top. We may be overcome by weakness for a season with grave heaviness of mind, disputation of heart, and misunderstanding of God's action or allowing of what happened. But it will pass.

When the emotional state is frayed, rationality is stunted, stunned, shocked, and stymied. Upon the restoration of good judgment and trust in God, the wearied and wounded saint recovers. Charles Simeon says, "The workings of his mind, under all the trials and difficulties which he has to encounter, are here set forth. He is convinced that no created arm can be sufficient for him. Hence, he directs his eyes towards the Creator himself, and saith of him, 'He is my refuge' from every trouble."[350] See Psalm 91:2. Ultimately, he will say with Paul, "If God be for us, who can be against us" (Romans 8:31).

In the *breakdown*s of life, trust God's faithfulness until the *breakthroughs* come.

81 Bring Your Questions to God

"God is not afraid of our questions and doubts—in fact, He longs to answer them."[351] ~ David Jeremiah

What do we do when something happens that just doesn't make sense? We ask the plaguing, hard questions with reverence in search of understanding. Habakkuk did: "How long, LORD, must I call for help, but you do not listen? Or cry out to you, 'Violence!' but you do not save? Why do you make me look at injustice? Why do you tolerate wrongdoing?" (Habakkuk 1:2–3 NIV). Other biblical writers did likewise.

Questioning God, however, as to the why of a happening ought to be done with an attitude of reverence, not rashness (Ecclesiastes 5:2). It ought to be done inquiringly, not judgmentally (Romans 9:20). It ought to be done humbly, not arrogantly (Isaiah 55:8–9). It ought to be done searchingly, not derogatorily (Job 40:1–2). It ought not to be done trustingly, not skeptically (Acts 9:6). The right basis in questioning God is to gain His perspective on that which was allowed to happen in an effort to make some sense out of it and gain serenity through it (not unjustly accuse Him).

G. K. Chesterton states, "The beginning of questioning well is to seek to question well, which may mean laying down our questions and allowing them to be reshaped and reformed by the answers given us by God."[352] Mark Littleton said, "Turn your doubts into questions; turn your questions to prayers; turn your prayers to God."

Questions may or may not yield satisfying answers presently. Habakkuk failed to get the answers he sought to his questions in his head, yet God ministered to the hurts of his heart. "Having the answers," writes Ravi Zacharias, "is not essential to living. What is essential is the sense of God's presence during dark seasons of questioning."[353]

Beyond the loving inquiry of God, search the Scriptures for answers and avail yourself of the assistance of devout spiritual believers that have walked the same path. Payson, while experiencing serious bodily affliction was asked if he knew any specific reason for it. "No," he replied, "but I am as well satisfied as if I could see ten thousand; God's will is the very perfection of all reason."[354]

82   The Positive Side of Death

"Death to the Christian is the funeral of all his sorrows and evils, and the resurrection of all his joys."[355] ~ James H. Aughey

What do we do when something happens that just doesn't make sense, like the death of a family member or friend? Death seems senseless. It is named an enemy. It stops earthly pursuits and dreams. It is said to have a powerful stinger. It wounds and devastates lives. It attacks faith and hope. It ends earthly relationships. It refuses to be avoided. It creates void and emptiness in hearts. It seals from view what's beyond its door.

But Jesus says it's not without meaning and purpose, for it's the threshold that leads to life eternal in Heaven with Him and the all the saints. So, what do we do, when faced with a loved one's death that crushes the heart and is beyond our understanding? We remember that death possesses divine purpose and meaning for the Christian, the fullness of which at present cannot be fully comprehended or known. We remember that death is not a dead end but a thoroughfare into the presence of Almighty God and the joys He has prepared for us in Heaven with our family and friends. We remember the words of Spurgeon: "Death to the saints is not a penalty; it is not destruction; it is not even a loss. It is a privilege.[356] It is the very joy of this earthly life to think that it will come to an end."[357]

Max Lucado provides sage counsel. "In God's plan every life is long enough and every death is timely. And though you and I might wish for a longer life, God knows better. And—this is important—though you and I may wish a longer life for our loved ones, they don't. Ironically, the first to accept God's decision of death is the one who dies. While we are shaking heads in disbelief, they are lifting hands in worship. While we are mourning at a grave, they are marveling at Heaven. While we are questioning God, they are praising God."[358]

Thomas Brooks says, "A man that sees his *rightness and acceptance* in God knows that death shall be the funeral of all his sins, sorrows, afflictions, temptations, desertions, oppositions, vexations, oppressions, and persecutions. And he knows that death shall be the resurrection of his hopes, joys, delights, comforts, and contentments, and that it shall bring him to a more clear, full, perfect, and constant enjoyment of God."[359]

With such understanding of death and Christ's words, "I am the resurrection, and the life: he that believeth in me, though he were dead, yet shall he live" (John 11:25), much of the fog of death is cleared. John Stott said, "Of course dying can be very unpleasant, and bereave-ment can bring bitter sorrow. But death itself has been overthrown, and 'blessed are the dead who die in the Lord' (Revelation 14:13). The proper epitaph to write for a Christian believer is not a dismal and uncertain petition, 'R.I.P.' (*requiescat in pace:* 'may he rest in peace'), but a joyful and certain affirmation 'C.A.D.' ('Christ abolished death')."[360]

83   The Bible Is Not a Senseless Book

"Scientific accuracy confirms the Bible is the Word of God."[361]
~ Adrian Rogers

What do we do when something happens that just doesn't make sense, like being told the Bible is the divine revelation of God to man? We don't dismiss it. We study it, research it, explore it and investigate it to see if it is or not, the way Lee Strobel and others like him did (their research led to total belief that the Bible is the inspired, infallible Word of God and led to their conversion to Christ).

Totally true in fact and doctrine, the Bible contains no contradictions and is thoroughly trustworthy. W. A. Criswell states, "Through the Holy Spirit's agency, God is involved in both the production and interpretation of Scripture. Men of God in antiquity spoke as they were moved by the Holy Spirit. 'Moved' means literally 'to bear along.' Scripture is infallible precisely because the Holy Spirit 'bore along' the prophets who spoke and wrote."[362]

While the Bible validates itself through an array of internal supports of its reliability—consistency, multiple witnesses, verifiable history—the Bible is also validated by many external evidences. For instance, it has been confirmed by more than one hundred archeological finds and hundreds of fulfilled prophecies. The proof of the authority and validity of the Bible is available upon honest investigation and the ministry of the Holy Spirit.

Thomas Newberry (author of the Newberry Bible), just prior to his death, was asked if he had ever been tormented with doubts as to the inspiration of the Bible. He replied, "I have spent sixty years in the study of the Scriptures in the original languages, marking carefully every tense and preposition, and the impression left on my mind is not the difficulty of believing but the impossibility of doubting the inspiration of the Scriptures."[363] All who make a study of it hold the same belief.

84   The Resurrection of Jesus Is Not Senseless

"The resurrection of Jesus Christ. It's provable historically. It's undeniable philosophically and logically."[364] ~ Jon Courson

What do we do when something happens that just doesn't make sense, like Jesus' being raised from the dead? We don't dismiss it because it seems too incredible, but investigate it like Josh McDowell did. And the investigation will lead to its verification. The resurrection of Christ is a fact established by the clearest, verifiable evidence.

Roman soldiers (elite trained fighting men of the highest order) guarded Jesus' tomb to ensure a resurrection hoax couldn't be fabricated.

The stone that sealed Jesus' tomb weighed one and a half to two tons (approximate weight of a mid-size car)—far too huge for a few men to roll away at all, and certainly not without awakening the soldiers had they fallen asleep.

The Roman seal, which stood for the power and authority of the Roman Empire, was affixed to the tomb. Automatic execution by crucifixion upside down would be the lot of anyone who broke the seal.

The linen wrappings that had been placed on the body of Jesus were found in the tomb in a fashion that indicated Jesus simply passed through them. Obviously had thieves taken Jesus' body, these wrappings would have been in disarray.

The fact that *the Jews taught Jesus' body was stolen* in reality means they believed his tomb was empty.[365] The stolen body theory was circulated early on but discounted due to the tremendous safeguards by Pilate against such occurring—the gigantic stone, the seal, the trained Roman soldiers placed to guard it.

Further, such a claim actually doesn't compute, for forty days after the resurrection, friends and enemies both testify they saw Jesus alive.[366] *Jesus revealed Himself* to over 500 people before returning to Heaven (1 Corinthians 15:3–6).

Another evidence of Christ's resurrection is in *the change that was manifested in the disciples*. Prior to it, they were fearful and cowardly; but after seeing the risen Christ, they were bold and courageous in proclaiming the Gospel. The disciples would not have suffered and died (all but one died a martyr's death) for a known hoax. People don't die for what they know is a lie.

The historian Josephus refers to *the half-brother of Jesus,* whose name was James, as do both Mark and John in Scripture (Mark 3:31; 6:3–4; John 7:3–5). James was not a believer until Jesus appeared unto Him following His resurrection (1 Corinthians 15:7). He subsequently became a leader in the Jerusalem church and later a martyr.

The disciples were not alone in experiencing a change following the resurrection, for within weeks of the resurrection a community of *at least ten thousand Jews* gave up the very sociological and theological traditions that had given them their national identity.[367]

Jesus' fulfillment of the many prophecies concerning the Messiah made hundreds of years earlier provide the surest evidence of His identity and resurrection. "God told us before it happened (through prophecies), so we might believe it after it happened." "On one single day of twenty-four hours, from the time of Christ's arrest in Gethsemane to the hour when He was buried in the shadow of the cross, no less than half a hundred specific prophecies were fulfilled! Any mathematician will tell you that the numerical chance of accidental fulfillment would run into astronomical figures against it. Just to mention a few, four classes of people were to be active in the crucifixion (Psalm 2:1–2). Christ was to be sold for silver, betrayed by a friend, forsaken by disciples. The betrayer would eat bread at a table with Him. His hands and feet would be pierced. He would drink vinegar and gall. They would cast lots for His vesture. The price of betrayal would go to the potter's field. What of those prophecies? Were they fulfilled? They were fulfilled…accurately."[368] Noting these proofs of Christ's resurrection, "Why should it be thought a thing incredible with you, that God should raise the dead?" (Acts 26:8). It isn't as senseless as the world would have us believe, is it?

85   The Problem with Evil

"God would never permit evil, if He could not bring good out of evil."[369] ~ Augustine

What do we do when something happens that just doesn't make sense? We remember that prior to the fall of Adam, everything made sense, that man's sin was the game-changer. A. W. Pink said, "There is a Holy Trinity, and there is likewise a Trinity of Evil."[370]

John MacArthur explains, "All evil in the universe emanates from the sins of fallen creatures. For example, Romans 5:12 says that death entered the world because of sin. Death, pain, disease, stress, exhaustion, calamity, and all the bad things that happen came as a result of the entrance of sin into the universe (Genesis 3:14–24). All those evil effects of sin continue to work in the world and will be with us as long as sin is."[371] That is why senseless, bad and devastating things happen to us and in our world. In understanding this fact, the senseless really becomes sensible.

"Have you ever wondered," asked Adrian Rogers, "why God doesn't obliterate the Devil and eradicate all sin? If God destroyed evil, God would destroy every opportunity of choice, for we would no longer have the freedom to choose good over evil. And if God were to destroy every opportunity for choice, then God would destroy every opportunity for us to choose freely to love. Therefore, God would destroy the highest good. For God to destroy evil would be evil. God doesn't destroy evil; instead, God defeats evil. How? Through Calvary and the resurrection, God turns every hurt into a hallelujah, every defeat into victory!"[372]

The good news is that paradise lost will one day be regained. Evil, though present, is only temporary. Upon Christ's return to earth, evil will be eternally banished—no more tears, sorrow, suffering, sickness or death—and "the wolf and the lamb shall feed together" (Isaiah 65:25). What a glorious day that will be!

86 When It Doesn't Make Sense, Praise God Anyhow

"The deepest level of worship is praising God in spite of pain, thanking God during a trial, trusting Him when tempted, surrendering while suffering, and loving Him when He seems distant. At my lowest, God is my hope. At my darkest, God is my light. At my weakest, God is my strength. At my saddest, God is my comforter."[373] ~ Rick Warren

What do we do when something happens that just doesn't make sense? We praise God. In the midst of chaos, confusion and despair over his grave loss, Habakkuk decided to praise and worship God even when it didn't make sense (Habakkuk 3:17–18). He said, "I'm singing joyful praise to GOD. I'm turning cartwheels of joy to my Savior God" (Habakkuk 3:18 MSG).

What are the benefits of praising God when it doesn't make sense? *Praise boosts the spirit.* Praise has the power to lift the spirit of heaviness. God promises the saint a great exchange: "the garment of praise for the spirit of heaviness" (Isaiah 61:3). The "garment of praise" literally means to be "wrapped up in praise." Wrap or envelop your soul in continual praise to God, and the depressing and oppressing spirit of heaviness will vanish.

Praise fixes our gaze upon Christ. Praise turns the focus away from the problem, recentering it upon the Savior who stands ready to meet us at our point of need.

Praise brings joy. The psalmist praise filled his "heart and flesh" with joy (see Psalm 71:23).

Praise strengthens and enlarges faith. Romans 4:20 says, Abraham "grew strong and was empowered by faith as he gave praise and glory to God" (AMPC).

Praise bolsters security. Praise prompts recollection that there is nothing too hard or difficult to endure, thwart or accomplish with God in the equation.

Praise calms the soul. Praise repels disquietude, anxiety and fear (Psalm 23:2).

Praise alters perspective. Praise enables us to see our present hardship, sorrow or sickness in light of God's omnipotence, love and sovereignty.

Praise drives Satan back. Praise thwarts the Devil's efforts to discourage, despair, depress, dissuade and defeat us. Mary Slessor, a godly missionary with the Chinese, said, "I sing the Doxology and dismiss the Devil."[374]

87 Appropriating of Faith

"Let God's promises shine on your problems."[375] ~ Corrie Ten Boom

What do we do when something happens that just doesn't make sense? We are to appropriate faith with regard to the promises of God, making them our personal possession. A small child was asked to explain what appropriating faith meant. He answered, "It is taking a pencil and underlining every 'me,' 'my' and 'mine' in the Bible." However, he should also have added, "And then it is taking those promises to God, claiming their payment in faith."

Search the Scriptures for the promises of God, and upon each that you find write, "This promise is mine."Then appropriate it by faith (make a withdrawal from the bank of Heaven for it). Put God in *remembrance of His promises* in times of the inexplicables of life (distress, difficulty, death, defeat, discouragement and danger), for in this, faith is exhibited and God is pleased. Spurgeon said, "The best praying man is the man who is most believingly familiar with the promises of God. After all, prayer is nothing but taking God's promises to Him, and saying to Him, 'Do as Thou hast said.' Prayer is the promise utilized. A prayer which is not based on a promise has no true foundation."[376]

W. S. Plumer says, "God will never disappoint expectations authorized and encouraged by His own promises."[377]

W. A. Criswell said, "When our trials come, when we feel pain and suffering, when our tears flow again, it is our joy and comfort to lift our faces Heavenward and to go on, standing on the promises of God."[378] *God's promises are sure.* Jesus said that Heaven and earth may pass away, but that His Word would stand sure forever (Matthew 24:35). Not one of His promises has ever failed or will ever fail. All that He promised will come to pass, including that which affirms that good will come out of the bad and senseless things that happen to those that love Him (Romans 8:28).

88 Salvation Is Too Good to Be True

"The name Emmanuel takes in the whole mystery. Jesus is 'God with us.' He had a nature like our own in all things, sin only excepted. But though Jesus was 'with us' in human flesh and blood, He was at the same time very God."[379] ~ J. C. Ryle

What do we do with something that just doesn't make sense, like Jesus' death, burial and resurrection for man's eternal redemption? It sounds like good news, but is it a little too good to be true?

What we believe about Jesus impacts all of life and myriad decisions. Neutral we cannot be with regard to His identity. Either Jesus was a legend (never existed), a liar (claimed to be the Son of God that came to earth on a redemptive mission), a lunatic ("on the level with the man who says he is a poached egg") or He is Lord, as He proclaimed (Matthew 27:43). Oswald Chambers said, "Jesus Christ became incarnate for one purpose, to make a way back to God that man might stand before Him as He was created to do, the friend and lover of God Himself."[380]

How might a person know the truth of Jesus? Jesus Himself gives answer in John 7:17: "If anyone is willing to do His will, he will know whether the teaching is of God or whether I speak on My own accord and by My own authority" (AMP). That is, if a man really wants to know and do the will of God, God will reveal Himself to him through honest and serious investigation of Holy Scripture. The condition of the inquiry is willingness to obey the truth revealed. It is to honestly say, "God, if you exist, if this is Your Word, if it is true, reveal it to me, and I will follow it wherever it leads me. If you don't convince me that it is true, I will continue the same way I am."[381] I don't know of anyone that honestly did this who did not walk away a follower of Jesus Christ.

"How many people would it take flipping a quarter before one person hits heads thirty times in a row? According to *Ripley's Believe It or Not! Strange Coincidences*, 'In order for a coin to land on heads fifty times in a row, it would take one million men flipping ten coins a minute forty hours a week; and then it would happen only once every nine hundred years.' There are at least thirty prophecies about the birth, the death, and the resurrection of the Messiah that were fulfilled in Jesus Christ. Wouldn't you agree that's a whole lot like tossing a coin thirty times in a row and having it come up heads?"[382] Declared Norman Geisler, "All the evidence points to Jesus as the divinely appointed fulfillment of the Messianic prophecies. He was God's Man, confirmed by God's signs."[383] Though Jesus and the salvation He offers sound too good to be true, they are not. C. S. Lewis says, "You must make your choice. Either this Man was, and is, the Son of God, or else a madman or something worse."[384]

89 When God Tells You to Do Something That Seems Senseless

"Faith is following God's instructions, even when they don't make sense, even when they don't seem logical or rational. Faith means being obedient."[385] ~ Rick Warren

What do we do when God tells us something to do that just doesn't make sense, like the instruction to Abraham to sacrifice his son Isaac on Mount Moriah? We in faith, without arguing or asking for explanations, obey as Abraham did

(Genesis 22:3–10). Matthew Henry says, "Faith had taught him [Abraham] not to argue, but to obey. He is sure that what God commands is good, that what He promises cannot be broken. In matters of God, whoever consults with flesh and blood will never offer up his Isaac to God."[386]

Spurgeon reveals the reason for the instruction. "Abraham was a man whose life gave good evidence of his faith in Jehovah, but the Lord is a jealous God, and He loves to have still more evidence of the fidelity of His people. He hungers after clear proofs from them that they really are His, and He works in them by His grace until He casts out all other loves, and all other confidences, that He may have the whole of their hearts, and that they may love Him and trust Him supremely."[387] So the account was a test of Abraham's obedience (would he so trust God that he would do as He commanded and slay his own son?), a test he passed with flying colors.

"God is to this man a friend to be trusted; to be loved better than an only son; to be obeyed where reason refuses its light to justify the command, and nature with all her voices can only exclaim against it."[388] It reveals that behind the "senseless" things we are asked of God to do there is "rhyme and reason" (divine purpose and design). The key is to exhibit unreserved trust in God, no matter how foolish, ludicrous or senseless the act *seems* that He beckons to be done.

Others may say we are acting foolhardily when we do, but they said that of the choicest of God's saints who dared to trust and obey God in the past with regard to vocational Christian service, missionary endeavors and expeditions, financial ministry investments, and the sacrificing of earthly pleasures to serve the living God.

John MacArthur says, "The account of Abraham tells us that a man can go through the severest trial of life imaginable if he really trusts God, believing that He will keep His promise and accomplish His purposes without making mistakes."[389] MacArthur continues, "Trials test our love for God by how we react to them. If we supremely love God, we will thank God for what He is accomplishing through them. But if we love ourselves more than God, we will question God's wisdom and become upset and bitter."[390]

90 The Bottom Line about the Senseless

"God knows better than we do. He always does—even when it doesn't make sense."[391] ~ Karen Kingsbury

What do we do when something happens that just doesn't make sense? We ask God for discernment as to why it happened, in search for answers. "Searching for God's answers and learning to view 'bad things' as 'good things in disguise' are disciplines that God wants His children to develop as they mature spiritually."[392] We understand that nothing happens to God's children without His allowance, therefore we rest in confidence that the bad will always be used for good in some way, by some means (Romans 8:28). Alexander Maclaren said, "The poison is wiped off the arrow, though the arrow may mercifully wound; and the evil in the evil is all dissipated."[393] We understand that suffering and pain are the result of the curse of sin; that Adam's sin opened the door to evil to work havoc on earth which produces heartache, misery, and horrendous pain (Romans 5:12). Prior to sin's invasion of earth, man knew no violence, misery, heartache, death, suffering or tears. But paradise lost will be regained at Jesus' return. We realize that God's ways may be secretive (Deuteronomy 29:29), incomprehensible (Romans 11:33), and past searching out (Psalm 145:3).

What are we to do when the inexplicables of life occur? We exhibit unflinching trust in Him who loves us with an everlasting love. We acknowledge that God foresees the future and allows a seemingly senseless death to occur to preserve His child from greater evil and harm. We realize that when man is not prudent in His ways, mishap occurs. Solomon said, "A prudent person foresees danger and takes precautions. The simpleton goes blindly on and suffers the consequences" (Proverbs 22:3 NLT). We don't let Satan off the hook, knowing that he, not God, is the instigator of evil and wrong that brings destruction, despair and disappointment. We choose to walk by faith, not misguided emotions or worldly rationale. We face the fact that bad things happen to good people at times because of the influence of evil and ungodly friends (Proverbs 13:20) and acts of wicked parents (2 Kings 16:2–4).

When senseless things happen, what is to be our response? We don't doubt in the night that which we believed in the light about God. We seek to discover how we might turn our pain into gain to assist others and magnify Christ. We endeavor to respond to the bad as did our Savior when He experienced seemingly senseless grief, suffering and torment unjustly for us (Isaiah 53:7). We lean upon other believers for aided strength and support, especially those that have walked the path we are traveling. We rest upon the riches of His grace for comfort and consolation (Hebrews 4:16). We anchor ourselves to the Word of God and incessantly feed upon its promises and truths that nourish the soul with hope, comfort and guidance. We look at the trial through the lens of Heaven, not that of the world (Jeremiah 29:11). We keep singing our song of hope despite the sorrow. We look forward to the day when the inexplicables of life will be explained, the fog removed from our minds, and all is understood with clarity.

A day is coming when all the senselessness of life will make sense. We embrace the view that "nothing that brings a man nearer to God can be an enemy."[394] With Spurgeon, we learn to kiss the waves that batter our life that drive us to the throne of God pleading for grace in time of need. When God instructs us to do what appears to be senseless or foolish, like the sacrificing of our Isaac, we trust Him and do it over the inner and outer voices that urge us not to obey.

What we must not do is allow Satan to use the seemingly senseless happenings to drive a wedge between

God and us. Sorrow can either sweeten or sour our disposition with God. Choose not to become embittered toward God. Don't allow suffering and pain to drive you from the source of hope and help, but closer to it, to God. James Dobson states, "Satan wants you to give up on God, who seems to have lost control of your circumstances. But I urge you not to leave the safety of His protection. The Captain knows what He is doing."[395]

In the hour of trial,
        Jesus, plead for me,
Lest by base denial
        I depart from Thee.

When Thou seest me waver,
        With a look recall,
Nor for fear or favor
        Suffer me to fall.

Should Thy mercy send me
        Sorrow, toil, and woe,
Or should pain attend me
        On my path below,

Grant that I may never
        Fail Thy hand to see;
Grant that I may ever
        Cast my care on Thee.

When the last hour cometh,
        Fraught with strife and pain,
When Thou, Lord, returneth
        To the earth again,

On Thy truth relying
        As that hour draws near,
Jesus, take me, waiting,
        To Thy presence dear.
        ~ James Montgomery (1771–1854)

[1] https://journeyonline.org/never-doubt-in-the-dark-what-god-told-you-in-the-light/, accessed October 1, 2021.

[2] Needham, George C. *The Life and Labors of Charles H. Spurgeon.* (Boston: D. L. Guernsey, 1887), 7.

[3] Packer, J. I. *Knowing God.* (Downers Grove, IL: IVP Books, 1973), Front matter.

[4] Why Does God Allow Suffering? https://www.davidjeremiah.org/makingsense/suffering/why-does-god-allow-suffering?devdate=2021-03-23, accessed October 25, 2021.

[5] Spurgeon, C. H. "God's Thoughts and Ways Far Above Ours" (Sermon delivered December 2, 1877). https://www.spurgeon.org/resource-library/sermons/gods-thoughts-and-ways-far-above-ours/#flipbook/, accessed September 28, 2021.

[6] Bridges, Jerry. *Trusting God,* (Colorado Springs: Navpress, 1988), 29.

[7] https://quotestats.com/topic/when-god-doesnt-make-sense-quotes/, accessed September 16, 2021.

[8] https://quotestats.com/topic/when-god-doesnt-make-sense-quotes/, accessed September 16, 2021.

[9] Murphy, R. E. *Proverbs* (Vol. 22). (Dallas: Word, Incorporated, 1998), 191.

[10] https://wisdomquotes.com/faith-quotes/, accessed October 15, 2021.

[11] Spurgeon, C. H. "Christ's Hospital" (Sermon delivered March 9, 1890).

[12] Laurie, Greg. Devotion: "For Righteousness Sake," March 01, 2019. https://harvest.org/resources/devotion/for-righteousness-sake-2019/, accessed April 10, 2021.

[13] Moody, W. R., Ed., *Record of Christian Work,* Volume 36. (East Northfield, Massachusetts, 1917), 505.

[14] Bridges, Charles. *Exposition of the Book of Proverbs.* (Carlisle, PA: Banner of Truth Trust, 2008), 24.

[15] Buzzell, S. S. *The Bible Knowledge Commentary: An Exposition of the Scriptures* (Vol. 1), Proverbs, J. F. Walvoord and R. B. Zuck (Eds.). (Wheaton, IL: Victor Books, 1985), 911.

[16] Exell, J. S. *Proverbs.* (New York; Chicago; Toronto: Fleming H. Revell Company, n. d.), 56.

[17] Winslow, Octavius. *The Sympathy of Christ,* Chapter 5, "The Silence of Christ." [Although these words were speaking of the unexplainable things of God and His Word to the sinner, they are applicable to the seemingly bizarre and senseless happenings of life.]

[18] Spence-Jones, H. D. M. (Ed.). *Proverbs.* (London; New York: Funk & Wagnalls Company, 1909), 55.

[19] Ibid.

[20] Clarke, Adam. *Commentary on the Bible.* (1831), Proverbs 3:5.

[21] Simeon, C. *Horae Homileticae: Chronicles to Job* (Vol. 4). (London: Samuel Holdsworth, 1836), 485.

[22] Henry, M. Matthew Henry's Commentary on the Whole Bible: Complete and Unabridged in One Volume. (Peabody: Hendrickson, 1994), 959.

[23] https://www.wow4u.com/qfaith/, accessed October 14, 2021.

[24] Spurgeon, C. H. *The Treasury of David: Psalms 56-87* (Vol. 3). (London; Edinburgh; New York: Marshall Brothers, n.d.), 327.

[25] Ibid.

[26] Ibid, 325.

[27] Ibid, 329.

[28] Spurgeon, C. H. *Psalms.* (Wheaton, IL: Crossway Books, 1993), 328.

[29] Bridges, Jerry. *Trusting God,* 1988, 37.

[30] Exell, J. S. *The Biblical Illustrator: The Psalms* (Vol. 3). (New York; Chicago; Toronto; London; Edinburgh: Fleming H. Revell Company; Francis Griffiths, 1909), 392.

[31] Packer, J. I. *Knowing God.* (Downers Grove, IL: IVP Books, 1973).

[32] Morgan, R. J. *Nelson's Annual Preacher's Sourcebook,* 2002 Edition. (Nashville: Thomas Nelson Publishers, 2001), 397.

[33] Morgan, R. J. *Nelson's Complete Book of Stories, Illustrations, and Quotes* (electronic ed.). (Nashville: Thomas Nelson Publishers, 2000), 767.

[34] Spurgeon, C. H. "God's Thoughts and Ways Far Above Ours" (Sermon preached December 2, 1877). https://www.spurgeon.org/resource-library/sermons/gods-thoughts-and-ways-far-above-ours/#flipbook/, accessed September 28, 2021.

[35] Adrian Roges. The Possibility of Miracles (Wheaton, Ill: Crossway Books, 1997), 16.

[36] Morgan, R. J. *Nelson's Annual Preacher's Sourcebook,* 2002 Edition. (Nashville: Thomas Nelson Publishers, 2001), 397.

[37] Jennings, A. C. and W. H. Lowe. *The Psalms, with Introductions and Critical Notes* (Second Edition, Vol. 1). (London: Macmillan and Co., 1884), 134.

[38] Exell, J. S. *The Biblical Illustrator: The Psalms* (Vol. 2). (New York; Chicago; Toronto; London; Edinburgh: Fleming H. Revell Company; Francis Griffiths, 1909), 99.

[39] *The Spurgeon Study Bible,* 716.

[40] Plumer, W. S. *Studies in the Book of Psalms: Being a Critical and Expository Commentary, with Doctrinal and Practical Remarks on the Entire Psalter*. (Philadelphia; Edinburgh: J. B. Lippincott Company; A & C Black, 1872), 389.

[41] Rogers, Adrian. "Outrageous Hope, Extravagant Joy." https://www.bellevue.org/wp-content/uploads/Week-8-Lecture-notes.pdf, accessed June 21, 2020.

[42] Packer, J. I. *The J. I. Packer Classic Collection*. (Colorado Springs: NavPress, 2010), 86.

[43] https://quotefancy.com/quote/1670103, accessed October 1, 2021.

[44] https://www.oneplace.com/ministries/love-worth-finding/read/devotionals/love-worth-finding/love-worth-finding-april-11-2014-11710521.html, accessed October 1, 2021.

[45] Cowman, L. B. *Streams in the Desert*. (Grand Rapids: Zondervan, 1996), January 14.

[46] Chen, Francis and Preston Sprinkle. *Erasing Hell: What God Said about Eternity, and the Things We've Made Up*. (Colorado Springs: David C. Cook, 2011), Chapter 5.

[47] Wuest, K. S. *Wuest's Word Studies from the Greek New Testament: for the English reader* (Vol. 2). (Grand Rapids: Eerdmans, 1997), 202–203.

[48] Ibid.

[49] Dobson, James. *When God Doesn't Make Sense*. (Wheaton: Tyndale, 1991).

[50] MacDonald, W. *Believer's Bible Commentary: Old and New Testaments*, (A. Farstad, Ed.) (Nashville: Thomas Nelson, 1995), 1728.

[51] Henry, M. Matthew Henry's Commentary on the Whole Bible: Complete and Unabridged in One Volume. (Peabody: Hendrickson, 1994), 2225.

[52] Spurgeon, C. H. "God's Thoughts and Ways Far Above Ours" (Sermon delivered December 2, 1877). https://www.spurgeon.org/resource-library/sermons/gods-thoughts-and-ways-far-above-ours/#flipbook/, accessed September 15, 2021.

[53] https://www.christianquotes.info/quotes-by-topic/quotes-about-trials/, accessed October 22, 2021.

[54] The quote is attributed to Spurgeon without documentation. He may have included it in a sermon or voiced it verbally to a friend that passed it along. Something similar is documented by the great British pastor in a sermon on record. "The wave of temptation may even wash you higher up upon the Rock of Ages, so that you cling to it with

a firmer grip than you have ever done before; and so again where sin abounds, grace will much more abound."

55 Spurgeon, C. H. *Spurgeon's Sermons,* Vol. 17: 1871. (Woodstock, Ontario, Canada: Devoted Publishing, 2017), 200.
56 Spurgeon, C. H. *Morning and Evening,* October 3 (Evening).
57 Spurgeon, C. H. *Morning and Evening,* October 16 (Evening).
58 https://www.crosswalk.com/devotionals/daily-hope-with-rick-warren/daily-hope-with-rick-warren-march-24-2018.html
59 Spurgeon, C. H. *The Treasury of David: Psalms 120–150* (Vol. 6). (London; Edinburgh; New York: Marshall Brothers, n.d.), 263.
60 https://www.pinterest.com/pin/351210470919131893/, accessed September 18, 2021.
61 Jeremiah, David. "No Surprises!" https://www.davidjeremiah.org/magazine/article/no-surprises-231, accessed September 18, 2021.
62 Sibbes, Richard. *The Complete Works of Richard Sibbes,* Vol. VII (Edinburgh: James Nichol, 1864), 200.
63 Exell, J. S. *The Biblical Illustrator: Isaiah* (Vol. 3). (New York; Chicago; Toronto; London; Edinburgh: Fleming H. Revell Company, n.d.), 21.
64 Exell, J. S. *The Biblical Illustrator: The Psalms,* Vol. 5. (New York; Chicago; Toronto; London; Edinburgh: Fleming H. Revell Company, n.d.), 182.
65 Exell, J. S. *The Biblical Illustrator: Exodus.* (New York; Chicago; Toronto; London; Edinburgh: Fleming H. Revell Company, n.d.), 307.
66 "Do All Things Work Together for Good?" Billy Graham Evangelistic Association, July 6, 2010. https://billygraham.org/story/do-all-things-work-together-for-good/, accessed July 25, 2020.
67 Exell, J. S. *The Biblical Illustrator: Romans* (Vol. 2). (New York; Chicago; Toronto; London; Edinburgh: Fleming H. Revell Company, n.d.), 153.
68 MacArthur, John. *The MacArthur New Testament Commentary: Romans,* Vol. 1. (Chicago: Moody Press, 1991), 473.
69 Ibid.
70 Ibid.
71 Winslow, Octavius. *The Sympathy of Christ.* Chapter 7, "The Sensitiveness of Christ to Suffering."
72 Criswell, W. A. "God's Providential Care" (Sermon). October 24, 1954. https://wacriswell.com/sermons/1954/god-s-providential-care/, accessed August 22, 2020.
73 Lucado, Max. *One God, One Plan, One Life.*
74 Morgan, R. J. *Nelson's Annual Preacher's Sourcebook,* 2002 Edition. (Nashville: Thomas Nelson Publishers, 2001), 397.

[75] Spurgeon, C. H. "Now and Then" (Sermon delivered 1871). https://www.spurgeon.org/resource-library/sermons/now-and-then/#flipbook/, accessed October 10, 2021.

[76] Cowman, L. B. *Streams in the Desert.* (Grand Rapids: Zondervan, 1997), July 25.

[77] https://www.preceptaustin.org/hebrews_111-2, accessed April 9, 2022.

[78] Spurgeon, C. H. *Morning and Evening,* May 31 (Evening).

[79] Warren, Rick. "Inspirational Sayings." https://www.wow4u.com/qfaith/, accessed October 14, 2021.

[80] Chambers, Oswald. *My Utmost for His Highest,* April 21. Author's paraphrase.

[81] Exell, J. S. *The Biblical Illustrator: Isaiah* (Vol. 2). (New York; Chicago; Toronto; London; Edinburgh: Fleming H. Revell Company, n.d.), 275.

[82] https://gracequotes.org/topic/god-sovereignty/, accessed November 10, 2021.

[83] Potts, James H. *Living Thoughts of John Wesley.* (New York: Hunt & Eaton, 1891), 297.

[84] https://www.gracegems.org/06/10/trials.html, accessed September 30, 2021.

[85] Barratt, Alfred (1879–1968). "Jesus Is Holding My Hand"

[86] Exell, J. S. *The Biblical Illustrator: Isaiah* (Vol. 2). (New York; Chicago; Toronto; London; Edinburgh: Fleming H. Revell Company, n.d.), 283.

[87] Precept Austin. The Hand of the Lord. https://www.preceptaustin.org/the_hand_of_the_lord, accessed January 16, 2021.

[88] Alcorn, Randy. *God's Promise of Happiness.* (Carol Streams, ILL: Tyndale House Publishers, 2015), 83.

[89] Exell, J. S. *The Biblical Illustrator: Isaiah* (Vol. 2). (New York; Chicago; Toronto; London; Edinburgh: Fleming H. Revell Company, n.d.), 277.

[90] *The Biblical Illustrator.* Isaiah 41:13–14.

[91] Spurgeon, C. H. *Morning and Evening,* October 21 (Evening).

[92] Swanson, J. *Dictionary of Biblical Languages with Semantic Domains: Hebrew (Old Testament)* (electronic ed.). (Oak Harbor: Logos Research Systems, Inc., 1997).

[93] Simeon, C. *Horae Homileticae: Isaiah, XXVII–LXVI* (Vol. 8). (London: Holdsworth and Ball, 1832), 142.

[94] *The Pulpit Commentary,* "The Eternal God a Refuge" (Deuteronomy 33:27).

[95] https://biblehub.com/sermons/luke/2-25.htm.

[96] Exell, J. S. *The Biblical Illustrator: Isaiah* (Vol. 3). (New York; Chicago; Toronto; London; Edinburgh: Fleming H. Revell Company, n.d.), 18.

[97] Piper, John, and Justin Taylor (eds.). *Suffering and the Sovereignty of God.* (Wheaton, Ill: Crossway Books, 2006), 166.

[98] Exell, J. S. *The Biblical Illustrator: The Psalms* (Vol. 3). (New York; Chicago; Toronto; London; Edinburgh: Fleming H. Revell Company; Francis Griffiths, 1909), 392.

[99] Ibid.

[100] https://quotestats.com/topic/quotes-about-the-big-picture/, accessed October 7, 2021.

[101] Spurgeon, C. H. *Metropolitan Tabernacle Pulpit,* Volume 17. "Now and Then." https://www.spurgeon.org/resource-library/sermons/now-and-then/#flipbook/, accessed October 10, 2021.

[102] Spurgeon, C. H. https://www.preceptaustin.org/the_attributes_of_god_-_spurgeon, accessed October 7, 2021.

[103] MacLaren, Alexander. *Expositions of Holy Scripture,* Psalm 43:5.

[104] Boice, J. M. *Psalms 42–106: An Expositional Commentary.* (Grand Rapids, MI: Baker Books, 2005), 370.

[105] Ibid.

[106] Quotefancy. "Top 500 Dietrich Bonhoeffer Quotes," (2021 Update), accessed September 21, 2021.

[107] Winslow, Octavius. *The Sympathy of Christ,* Chapter 5: "The Silence of Christ."

[108] Spurgeon, C. H. "The Unrivalled Friend." (Sermon delivered November 7, 1869).

[109] Morgan, G. Campbell. *The Westminster Pulpit,* Vol. 4. (Grand Rapids: Baker Book House, 2006), 194.

[110] "Waiting When God Seems Silent," FEBRUARY 10, 2019. https://www.desiringgod.org/articles/waiting-when-god-seems-silent, accessed October 6, 2021.

[111] Winslow, Octavius. *The Sympathy of Christ,* Chapter 5: "The Silence of Christ."

[112] Spurgeon, C. H. "For the Troubled" (Sermon delivered January 12, 1873). http://spurgeongems.org/sermon/chs1090.pdf, accessed September 28, 2021.

[113] Schultz, Lynda. "The Story Behind the Song," adapted. https://www.thrive-magazine.ca/blog/40/, accessed September 17, 2021.

[114] Sibbes, Richard, adapted.

[115] Henry, M. Matthew Henry's Commentary on the Whole Bible: Complete and Unabridged in One Volume. (Peabody: Hendrickson, 1994), 1154.

[116] Hayford, Jack, and Dick Eastman. *Living and Praying in Jesus' Name.* (Wheaton, Ill: Tyndale House Publishers, 1988), 128.

[117] Clowney, Edmund. https://www.christianquotes.info/images/3-reasons-trials/, accessed October 25, 2021.

[118] Hodge, Charles. *A Commentary on the Epistle to the Ephesians.* (Baker Book House, 1980), 389.

[119] MacArthur, John. "Spiritual Warfare: Who's After Whom?" from *Our Sufficiency in Christ.* (Wheaton, Illinois: Crossway Books, a division of Good News Publishers, 1991), 235.

[120] Wiersbe, W. W. *Be Patient.* (Wheaton, IL: Victor Books, 1996), 94–95.

[121] Wuest, K. S. *Wuest's Word Studies from the Greek New Testament: for the English Reader,* (Vol. 5) (Grand Rapids: Eerdmans, 1997), 74.

[122] McConkey, James. *The Three-Fold Secret of the Holy Spirit.* (Pittsburgh, PA: Silver Publishing Society, 1975), 65–66.

[123] Simeon, C. *Horae Homileticae: Philippians to 1 Timothy* (Vol. 18). (London: Holdsworth and Ball, 1833), 69.

[124] Spurgeon, C. H. *Morning and Evening,* October 7 (Morning)

[125] Criswell, W. A. "Trusting God." Daily Word, November 22, 2017. W. A. Criswell Sermon Library.

[126] Allen, Kerry James. *Exploring the Mind and Heart of the Prince of Preachers.* (Oswego, IL: Fox River Press, 2005), 402.

[127] MacArthur, John. "Spiritual Warfare: Who's After Whom?" from *Our Sufficiency in Christ.* (Wheaton, Illinois: Crossway Books, a division of Good News Publishers, 1991), 230.

[128] Spurgeon, C. H. "Satan Considering the Saints" (Sermon delivered April 9, 1865). https://www.spurgeon.org/resource-library/sermons/satan-considering-the-saints/#flipbook/, accessed September 29, 2021.

[129] Ash, Christopher. *Job: The Wisdom of the Cross, Preaching the Word.* (Wheaton, IL: Crossway, 2014), 424.

[130] Craig D. Lounsbrough, An Intimate Collision: Encounters with Life and Jesus.

[131] Simeon, C. *Horae Homileticae: Psalms, LXXIII–CL* (Vol. 6). (London: Holdsworth and Ball, 1836), 392–393.

[132] Clarke, Adam. *Clarke's Commentary,* Psalm 125:2.

[133] Spurgeon, C. H. "God Is with Us" (Sermon delivered July 17, 1864).

[134] Keller, Tim. *Walking with God through Pain and Suffering.* (New York: Riverhead Books, 2015), 58.

[135] Spurgeon, C. H. "God Is with Us" (Sermon delivered July 17, 1864).

[136] Stiles, Wayne. *Waiting on God: What to Do When God Does Nothing.* (2015).

[137] Maclaren, Alexander. *Maclaren 's Expositions,* "Mountains Around Mount Zion," Psalm 125.

[138] Henry, M. Matthew Henry's Commentary on the Whole Bible: Complete and Unabridged in One Volume. (Peabody: Hendrickson, 1994), 932

[139] Plumer, W. S. *Studies in the Book of Psalms: Being a Critical and Expository Commentary, with Doctrinal and Practical Remarks on the Entire Psalter.* (Philadelphia; Edinburgh: J. B. Lippincott Company; A & C Black, 1872), 1109.

[140] Lincoln, Dick. "The Idols We Worship," sermon March 9, 2015. Shandon Baptist Church, Columbia, SC

[141] https://www.crosswalk.com/faith/spiritual-life/inspiring-quotes/ 31-prayer-quotes-be-inspired-and-encouraged.html, accessed September 17, 2021.

[142] https://www.azquotes.com/quote/815915, accessed September 28, 2021.

[143] "45 Charles Spurgeon Quotes to Uplift Your Faith Today," July 22, 2021. https://www.christianity.com/wiki/people/charles-spurgeon-quotes-to-uplift-your-faith-today.html, accessed September 28, 2021.

[144] Rogers, Adrian. "How to Pray for America," *Decision Magazine,* February 1, 2021.

[145] Bounds, E. M. *Purpose in Prayer,* XI.

[146] Rogers, Adrian. "Pesky Problems with Prayer: Frequently Asked Questions, Part 2," https://www.oneplace.com/ministries/love-worth-finding/read/articles/pesky-problems-with-prayer-18254.html, accessed October 15, 2021.

[147] Rogers, Adrian. *Adrian Rogers' Daily Devotionals.* "Your Infirmity May Reveal God's Glory," April 13.

[148] Rogers, Adrian. "When Prayer Seems Unanswered" (Sermon overview). https://www.lwf.org/sermons/audio/when-prayer-seems-unanswered-1550, accessed October 15, 2021.

[149] Ibid.

[150] https://quotes.pub/q/cast-not-away-your-confidence-because-god-defers-his-perform-602076, accessed July 13, 2020.

[151] https://gracequotes.org/quote/prayer-delights-gods-ear-it-melts-his-heart-and-opens-his-hand-god-cannot-deny-a-praying-soul/, accessed September 28, 2021.

[152] https://www.christianquotes.info/top-quotes/22-motivating-quotes-about-prayer/, accessed September 17, 2021.

[153] Blanchard, Charles. *Great Preaching on Prayer.* (Murfreesboro, TN: Sword of the Lord Publishers, 1988), 223–224.

154 Spurgeon, C. H. *The Treasury of David: Psalms 88–110* (Vol. 4). (London; Edinburgh; New York: Marshall Brothers, n.d.), 91.

155 Perowne, J. J. S. *The Book of Psalms: A New Translation, with Introductions and Notes, Explanatory and Critical* (Fifth Edition, Revised, Vol. 1). (London; Cambridge: George Bell and Sons; Deighton Bell and Co., 1883), 198.

156 Spurgeon, C. H. *The Treasury of David: Psalms 111–119* (Vol. 5). (London; Edinburgh; New York: Marshall Brothers, n.d.), 402.

157 Harman, A. *Psalms: A Mentor Commentary* (Vol. 1–2). (Ross-shire, Great Britain: Mentor, 2011), 176.

158 Spurgeon, C. H. *Psalms.* (Wheaton, IL: Crossway Books, 1993), 46.

159 https://www.christianquotes.info/top-quotes/16-glorious-quotes-promises-god/, accessed September 20, 2021.

160 https://www.ccel.org/ccel/spurgeon/checkbook.i.html, accessed September 24, 2021.

161 Ibid.

162 https://www.spurgeon.org/resource-library/sermons/gods-thoughts-and-ways-far-above-ours/#flipbook/, accessed September 26, 2021.

163 https://www.azquotes.com/quotes/topics/bad-things-happen.html, accessed September 28, 2021.

164 Spurgeon, C. H. "Faith's Ultimatum" (Sermon delivered July 18, 1885). https://www.spurgeon.org/resource-library/sermons/faiths-ultimatum/#flipbook/, accessed October 4, 2021.

165 Stanley, Charles. *Finding Peace.* (Nashville: Thomas Nelson, March 6, 2007), 6.

166 Elliot, Elizabeth. *Secure in the Everlasting Arms.* (Revell, 2004).

167 Spurgeon, C. H. "Beauty For Ashes" (Sermon published January 9, 1913).

168 Murray, Andrew. *Absolute Surrender.* (Springdale, PA: Whitaker House, 1981), 68.

169 Cowman, L. B. *Streams in the Desert.* (Grand Rapids: Zondervan, 1996), January 3.

170 Evans, Tony. "Has God Put More on You Than You Can Bear?" (Blog). https://tonyevans. org/has-god-put-more-on-you-than-you-can-bear/, accessed September 6, 2020.

171 https://www.christianquotes.info/quotes-by-topic/quotes-about-trials/, accessed October 22, 2021.

172 *Merriam-Webster Dictionary.*

173 https://www.pinterest.com/pin/11892386502016229/, accessed September 17, 2021.

[174] https://www.pinterest.com/pin/11892386502016229/, accessed September 17, 2021.

[175] Cowman, L. B. *Streams in the Desert*. (Grand Rapids: Zondervan, 1996), May 13.

[176] http://victoryminded.com/53-christian-quotes-on-hope-including-bible-verses/, accessed November 13, 2020.

[177] MacArthur, J., Jr. (Ed.). *The MacArthur Study Bible*. (electronic ed.). (Nashville, TN: Word Pub., 1997), 1824.

[178] Spurgeon, C. H. "Faith's Ultimatum" (Sermon delivered July 18, 1885). https://www.spurgeon.org/resource-library/sermons/faiths-ultimatum/#flipbook/, accessed October 4, 2021.

[179] https://www.azquotes.com/quote/783790, accessed October 4, 2021.

[180] Spurgeon, "The High Rock" (Sermon # 2728). New Park Street Chapel, 1859. https://www.spurgeongems.org/vols46-48/chs2728.pdf, accessed September 29, 2018.

[181] https://www.christianquotes.info/top-quotes/16-encouraging-quotes-about-hope/, accessed October 20, 2021.

[182] Spurgeon, "The High Rock" (Sermon # 2728). New Park Street Chapel, 1859. https://www.spurgeongems.org/vols46-48/chs2728.pdf, accessed September 29, 2018.

[183] Exell, J. S. *The Biblical Illustrator: Job*. (New York; Chicago; Toronto; London; Edinburgh: Fleming H. Revell Company, n.d.), 33.

[184] Wilkerson, David, "Have You Felt Like Giving Up Lately?"

[185] Cowman, L. B. *Streams in the Desert*. (Grand Rapids: Zondervan, 1996), February 7.

[186] Goodwin, Thomas. *The Works of Thomas Goodwin,* Vol. 1 (Edinburgh: James Nichol, 1861), 307.

[187] Maclaren, Alexander. *Maclaren's Expositions,* "The Answer to Trust," Psalm 91:14.

[188] Winslow, Octavius. *The Sympathy of Christ*. Chapter 7, "The Sensitiveness of Christ to Suffering."

[189] Bonar, Horatius. *Why God's Children Suffer*. (Chicago: Moody Press, 1845), Preface.

[190] Spurgeon, C. H. "Jehovah-Shammah" (Sermon delivered October 25, 1863). https://www.studylight.org/commentary/ezekiel/35-10.html, accessed October 14, 2021.

[191] https://whatisanything.com/what-is-an-oath-of-god/, accessed October 21, 2021.

[192] Cowman, L. B. *Streams in the Desert*. (Grand Rapids: Zondervan, 1996), February 14.

193 Spurgeon, C. H. *The Lost Sermons of C. H. Spurgeon,* Volume V. "The Coming of Spring," Sermon # 248, see point number 9.

194 Plumer, W. S. *Studies in the Book of Psalms: Being a Critical and Expository Commentary, with Doctrinal and Practical Remarks on the Entire Psalter.* (Philadelphia; Edinburgh: J. B. Lippincott Company; A & C Black, 1872), 183.

195 Spurgeon, C. H. *Psalms.* (Wheaton, IL: Crossway Books, 1993), 37.

196 Exell, J. S. *The Biblical Illustrator: Job.* (New York; Chicago; Toronto; London; Edinburgh: Fleming H. Revell Company, n.d.), 559.

197 Wiersbe, W. W. *Be Patient.* (Wheaton, IL: Victor Books, 1996), 136.

198 Maclaren, Alexander. *The Wearied Christ and Other Sermons.* (London: Alexander and Shepheard, 1893), 247.

199 Barnes, Albert. *Notes on the Bible,* (1834), Isaiah 61:3.

200 Spurgeon, C. H. "Beauty for Ashes," (Sermon published January 9, 1913.)

201 Barnes, Albert. *Notes on the Bible,* (1834), Psalm 30:5.

202 Simeon, C. *Horae Homileticae: Isaiah, XXVII–LXVI* (Vol. 8). (London: Holdsworth and Ball, 1832), 563.

203 Exell, J. S. *The Biblical Illustrator: Romans* (Vol. 1). (New York; Chicago; Toronto; London; Edinburgh: Fleming H. Revell Company, n.d.), 303.

204 Gill, John. *Exposition of the Entire Bible,* (1746–63), Romans 4:18.

205 Henry, Matthew. *Complete Commentary on the Whole Bible,* (1706), Romans 4:18.

206 Exell, J. S. *The Biblical Illustrator: Romans* (Vol. 1). (New York; Chicago; Toronto; London; Edinburgh: Fleming H. Revell Company, n.d.), 303.

207 *Life Worth Finding Daily Devotional,* "Have You Found That God Is Enough?" November 24, 2019.

208 https://rts.edu/resources/psalm-119-not-by-bread-alone-the-lord-is-my-portion/, accessed October 21, 2021.

209 Exell, J. S. *The Biblical Illustrator: The Lamentations of Jeremiah.* (London: Francis Griffiths, 1905), 55.

210 *Life Worth Finding Daily Devotional,* "Have You Found That God Is Enough?" November 24, 2019.

211 https://www.christianquotes.info/quotes-by-topic/quotes-about-compassion/, accessed September 28, 2021.

212 Spurgeon, C. H. *Morning and Evening,* September 28 (Morning).

213 Winslow, Octavius. *The Sympathy of Christ,* Chapter 2, "The Sigh of Christ," (1862).

214 Spurgeon, C. H. *Morning and Evening,* September 28 (Morning).

215 http://christian-quotes.ochristian.com/christian-quotes_ochristian.
cgi?find=Christian-quotes-by-Henry+Ward+Beecher-on-Trials,
accessed October 5, 2021.
216 https://www.christianquotes.info/quotes-by-topic/quotes-about-
compassion/, accessed September 28, 2021.
217 Exell, J. S. *The Biblical Illustrator: The Psalms* (Vol. 2). (New York;
Chicago; Toronto; London; Edinburgh: Fleming H. Revell Company;
Francis Griffiths, 1909), 97.
218 https://christianquote.com/peace-in-trouble/, accessed September
30, 2021.
219 Barnes, Albert. *Notes on the Bible,* (1834), Philippians 4:7.
220 Keller, Timothy. *Walking with God through Pain and Suffering.*
(London, Penguin Books, 2015).
221 Barnes, Albert. *Notes on the Bible,* (1834), John 14:27.
222 O'Brien, P. T. *The Epistle to the Philippians: A Commentary on the
Greek Text.* (Grand Rapids, MI: Eerdmans, 1991), 495–496.
223 Courson, J. *Jon Courson's Application Commentary.* (Nashville, TN:
Thomas Nelson, 2003), 557.
224 Spurgeon, C. H. "The Peace of God," (Sermon Delivered January 6,
1878). https://www.spurgeon.org/resource-library/sermons/the-
peace-of-god/#flipbook/, accessed September 21, 2021.
225 Spurgeon, C. H. "The Sweet Uses of Adversity." (Sermon delivered
November 13, 1859).
226 MacArthur, J., Jr. (Ed.). *The MacArthur Study Bible.* (electronic ed.).
(Nashville, TN: Word Pub., 1997), 1828
227 Wuest, K. S. *Wuest's Word Studies from the Greek New Testament:
for the English Reader* (Vol. 5). (Grand Rapids: Eerdmans,1997), 110.
228 MacArthur, J., Jr. (Ed.). *The MacArthur Study Bible.* (electronic ed.).
(Nashville, TN: Word Pub., 1997), 1828.
229 Wuest, K. S. *Wuest's Word Studies from the Greek New Testament:
for the English Reader* (Vol. 5). (Grand Rapids: Eerdmans,1997), 110.
230 Exell, J. S. *The Biblical Illustrator: Philippians–Colossians* (Vol. 1).
(New York; Chicago; Toronto; London; Edinburgh: Fleming H. Revell
Company, n.d.), 330.
231 Spurgeon, C. H. "The Peace of God." (Sermon Delivered January 6,
1878). https://www.spurgeon.org/resource-library/sermons/the-
peace-of-god/#flipbook/, accessed September 21, 2021.
232 McConkey, James. *The Three-Fold Secret of the Holy Spirit.*
(Pittsburgh, PA: Silver Publishing Society, 1975), 14–15.
233 Simeon, C. *Horae Homileticae: Psalms, I–LXXII* (Vol. 5). (London:
Holdsworth and Ball, 1836), 119).

[234] Ironside, H. A. *Studies on Book One of the Psalms*. (Neptune, NJ: Loizeaux Brothers, 1952), 130.

[235] Spurgeon, C. H. *Psalms*. (Wheaton, IL: Crossway Books, 1993), 73.

[236] Spurgeon, C. H. *Sermons on the Psalms: Unanswered Prayer*. (Grand Rapids: Zondervan Publishing House, 1960), 21.

[237] Spurgeon, C. H. *The Treasury of David: Psalms 1–26* (Vol. 1). (London; Edinburgh; New York: Marshall Brothers, n.d.), 303.

[238] Exell, J. S. *The Biblical Illustrator: Isaiah* (Vol. 3). (New York; Chicago; Toronto; London; Edinburgh: Fleming H. Revell Company, n.d.), 15.

[239] https://wisdomquotes.com/faith-quotes/, accessed October 15, 2021.

[240] Exell, J. S. *The Biblical Illustrator: Isaiah* (Vol. 3). (New York; Chicago; Toronto; London; Edinburgh: Fleming H. Revell Company, n.d.), 22.

[241] Gill, John. *Exposition of the Entire Bible,* (1746–63), Isaiah 50:10.

[242] Spurgeon, C. H. "Unstaggering Faith," (sermon delivered February 3, 1867). https://www.spurgeon.org/resource-library/sermons/unstaggering-faith/#flipbook/, accessed September 27, 2021.

[243] Exell, J. S. *The Biblical Illustrator: Job*. (New York; Chicago; Toronto; London; Edinburgh: Fleming H. Revell Company, n.d.), 556.

[244] Henry, M. Matthew Henry's Commentary on the Whole Bible: Complete and Unabridged in One Volume. (Peabody: Hendrickson, 1994), 726.

[245] Simeon, C. *Horae Homileticae: Chronicles to Job* (Vol. 4). (London: Holdsworth and Ball, 1836), 485.

[246] Henry, M. Matthew Henry's Commentary on the Whole Bible: Complete and Unabridged in One Volume. (Peabody: Hendrickson, 1994), 726

[247] Spurgeon, C. H. "Questions Which Ought to be Asked" (Sermon). https://answersingenesis.org/education/spurgeon-sermons/1511-questions-which-ought-to-be-asked/. Accessed September 28, 2021.

[248] Lewis, C. S. *The Joyful Christian*. (New York: Simon & Schuster, 1996), 134.

[249] https://www.azquotes.com/quotes/topics/sovereignty-of-god.html, accessed October 8, 2021.

[250] Spurgeon, C. H. *Morning and Evening,* December 19 (morning).

[251] "Table Talk on Trouble and Triumph," Part 1. The sermon originally appeared at: (https://www.gty.org/library/sermons-library/42-270/table-talk-on-trouble-and-triumph-part-1) at www.gty.org. © 1969-2008. Grace to You.

[252] Spence-Jones, H. D. M. (Ed.). *Proverbs*. (London; New York: Funk & Wagnalls Company, 1909), 321.

[253] David Jeremiah. "Knowing a Sovereign God" (Sermon), https://sermons.love/david-jeremiah/4065-david-jeremiah-knowing-a-sovereign-god.html, accessed October 7, 2021.

[254] Pink, Arthur W. *The Sovereignty of God,* 140.

[255] Spurgeon, C. H. https://www.preceptaustin.org/the_attributes_of_god_-_spurgeon, accessed October 7, 2021.

[256] Exell, J. S. *The Biblical Illustrator: I Kings.* (New York; Chicago; Toronto; London; Edinburgh: Fleming H. Revell Company, n.d.), 254.

[257] Ibid, 255.

[258] Jeremiah, David. "Job: Overcoming the Overwhelming" (Sermon). https://sermons.love/david-jeremiah/7541-david-jeremiah-job-overcoming-the-overwhelming.html, accessed October 14, 2021.

[259] Spurgeon, C. H. "Faith's Ultimatum" (Sermon delivered July 18, 1885). https://www.spurgeon.org/resource-library/sermons/faiths-ultimatum/#flipbook/, accessed October 8, 2021.

[260] Henry, M. Matthew Henry's Commentary on the Whole Bible: Complete and Unabridged in One Volume. (Peabody: Hendrickson, 1994), 756

[261] Exell, J. S. *The Biblical Illustrator: The Psalms* (Vol. 4). (New York; Chicago; Toronto; London; Edinburgh: Fleming H. Revell Company; Francis Griffiths, 1909), 78.

[262] Tozer, A. W. *The Knowledge of the Holy.*

[263] MacLaren, Alexander. *Expositions of Holy Scripture,* Job 22:21.

[264] Keller, Timothy. *Walking with God through Pain and Suffering.* (New York: Riverhead Books, 2013), 5.

[265] Ortlund, Eric. "Five Truths for Sufferers from the Book of Job." Volume 40, Issue 2. https://www.thegospelcoalition.org/themelios/article/five-truths-for-sufferers-from-the-book-of-job/, accessed October 16, 2021.

[266] Wiersbe, Warren W. *Why Us? When Bad Things Happen to God's People.* (Grand Rapids: Fleming H. Revell, 1984).

[267] Chambers, Oswald. *The Place of Help.* (Grand Rapids: Discovery House, 2015).

[268] Chambers, Oswald. *My Utmost for His Highest,* April 22.

[269] Horne, G. *A Commentary on the Book of Psalms.* (New York: Robert Carter & Brothers, 1856), 213–214.

[270] Spurgeon, C. H. *Morning and Evening,* September 1 (Evening).

[271] Spurgeon, C. H. "A Happy Christian," (sermon).

272 Spurgeon, C. H. *Morning and Evening.* (London: Passmore & Alabaster), October 7.

273 Ritzema, E., and E. Vince. (Eds.). *300 Quotations for Preachers from the Puritans.* (Bellingham, WA: Lexham Press, 2013).

274 Wiersbe, W. W. *With the Word Bible Commentary.* (Nashville: Thomas Nelson, 1991), Rev. 21:1.

275 MacArthur, J., Jr. (Ed.). *The MacArthur Study Bible.* (electronic ed.). (Nashville, TN: Word Pub., 1997), 2022.

276 *Funeral Sermons and Outlines.* (Grand Rapids: Baker Book House, 1955), 96.

277 Baxter, Richard. *The Saints' Everlasting Rest,* abridged by John T. Wilkinson. (London: Epworth, 1962), 110.

278 Coulter, Rachel. "Worshipping with a Broken Heart," January 8, 2017. https://www.desiringgod.org/articles/worshiping-with-a-broken-heart#modal-2597-sf9bshat, accessed October 17, 2021.

279 Kroll, Woodrow. https://www.christianquotes.info/quotes-by-topic/quotes-about-trials/, accessed October 22, 2021.

280 Exell, J. S. *The Biblical Illustrator: Isaiah* (Vol. 3). (New York; Chicago; Toronto; London; Edinburgh: Fleming H. Revell Company, n.d.), 370.

281 Spurgeon, C. H. "Christ's Hospital," (Sermon delivered March 9, 1890).

282 Ryle, J. C. *Holiness: Its Nature, Hindrances, Difficulties, and Roots.* (Peabody, MA: Hendriksen Publishers, 2007), 398.

283 https://www.dailychristianquote.com/g-campbell-morgan-21/, accessed April 9, 2022.

284 Cowman, L. B. *Streams in the Desert.* (Grand Rapids: Zondervan, 1996), January 14.

285 Spence-Jones, H. D. M. (Ed.). *Isaiah* (Vol. 2,). (London; New York: Funk & Wagnalls Company, 1910), 364.

286 Henry, Matthew. *Concise Commentary on the Whole Bible,* Isaiah 57:1.

287 Exell, J. S. *The Biblical Illustrator: Isaiah* (Vol. 3). (New York; Chicago; Toronto; London; Edinburgh: Fleming H. Revell Company, n.d.), 281.

288 Hamilton, William W. *Sermons on the Books of the Bible: Vol. 3,* 212.

289 Wiersbe, Warren W. *Bible Exposition Commentary: Old Testament Wisdom and Poetry.* (David C Cook, 2004), 486.

290 Spurgeon, C. H. *Morning and Evening,* October 21, Evening.

291 Swem, Edmond H. *Spurgeon's Gold: From the Works of C. H. Spurgeon.* (Washington: Judd & Detweiler, Printers, 1888), 162.

292 Lockyer, Herbert. *All the Promises of the Bible.* [The author says he discovered 7,147 promises from God to man in the Bible.]

293 MacArthur, John. *Safe in the Arms of God.* (Nashville: Thomas Nelson Publishers, 2003), 133–134.

294 MacArthur, John. *The MacArthur New Testament Commentary,* Ephesians 2:8–9.

295 Henry, M. Matthew Henry's Commentary on the Whole Bible: Complete and Unabridged in One Volume. (Peabody: Hendrickson, 1994), 1957.

296 https://www.azquotes.com/author/56255-Dave_Dravecky, accessed April 9, 2022.

297 Murray, Andrew. *Absolute Surrender.* (Springdale, PA: Whitaker House, 1981), 103.

298 Ibid, 99.

299 Ibid, 102–103.

300 Spurgeon, C. H. "Waking to See Christ's Glory" (Sermon delivered September 3, 1882). https://www.spurgeon.org/resource-library/ sermons/waking-to-see-christs-glory/#flipbook/, accessed November 1, 2021.

301 Murray, Andrew. *Absolute Surrender.* (Springdale, PA: Whitaker House, 1981), 106.

302 Ibid, 107.

303 Cowman, L. B. *Streams in the Desert.* (Grand Rapids: Zondervan, 1996), 387.

304 Ibid.

305 https://www.quotespedia.org/authors/a/anonymous/dont-worry-god-is-always-on-time-trust-him-anonymous/, accessed October 25, 2021.

306 Cowman, L. B. *Streams in the Desert.* (Grand Rapids: Zondervan, 1996), October 14.

307 Spurgeon, C. H. "Unstaggering Faith" (sermon delivered February 3, 1867). https://www.spurgeon.org/resource-library/sermons/ unstaggering-faith/#flipbook/, accessed September 27, 2021.

308 Truett, George W. *A Quest for Souls.* (New York and London: Harper & Brothers Publishers, 1917), 265, 267.

309 Redpath, Alan. *Alan Redpath Library: Lessons from the Life of David,* "The Making of a Man of God."

310 Rogers, Adrian. *The Possibility of Miracles.* (Illinois: Crossway Books, 1997), 18.

311 *The Biblical Illustrator,* John 11:25.

312 Rogers, Adrian. *The Possibility of Miracles.* (Illinois: Crossway Books, 1997), 17–18.

313 McConkey, James. *The Three-fold Secret of the Holy Spirit.* (Pittsburgh, PA: Silver Publishing Company, 1921), 34.

314 Ibid.

315 Ibid, 14.

316 Exell, J. S. *The Biblical Illustrator: Isaiah* (Vol. 3). (New York; Chicago; Toronto; London; Edinburgh: Fleming H. Revell Company, n.d.), 18.

317 https://welikequotes.com/author/william-cowper-1731/the-darkest-day-if-you-live-till-tomorrow-will-have-passed, accessed October 28, 2021.

318 Moody, W. R., (Ed.). *Record of Christian Work,* Volume 36. (East Northfield, Massachusetts, 1917), 505.

319 Lewis, C. S. *C. S. Lewis on Grief.* (Nashville: Thomas Nelson Publishers, 1998), Introduction.

320 Lewis, C. S. *A Grief Observed,* 1961, Chapter 2.

321 Lewis, C. S. *C. S. Lewis on Grief.* (Nashville: Thomas Nelson Publishers, 1998), 38.

322 Ibid., 39.

323 Ibid.

324 Knight, Walter B. *Knight's Illustrations for Today.* (Chicago: Moody Press, 1975), 93–94.

325 Ibid.

326 Chapell, Bryan. *The Hardest Sermons You'll Ever Have to Preach.* (Grand Rapids: Zondervan, 2011), 13.

327 Ibid, 14–15.

328 Bridges, Jerry. *Trusting God.* (NAVPRESS, 2008), 134.

329 Wiersbe, Warren. *Prayer, Praise and Promises.* (Grand Rapids: BakerBooks, 2011), 346.

330 Chapell, Bryan. *The Hardest Sermons You'll Ever Have to Preach.* (Grand Rapids: Zondervan, 2011), 223.

331 Wolterstorff, Nicholas. *Lament for a Son.* (Grand Rapids: Eerdmans, 1978), 81.

332 Spurgeon, C. H. "Waking to See Christ's Glory," (Sermon delivered September 3, 1882). https://www.spurgeon.org/resource-library/sermons/waking-to-see-christs-glory/#flipbook/, accessed November 1, 2021.

333 Spurgeon, C. H. *Psalms.* (Wheaton, IL: Crossway Books, 1993), 120.

334 Maclaren, Alexander. *The Book of Psalms,* 296.

[335] https://biblereasons.com/focusing-on-god/, accessed November 1, 2021.

[336] "Grow Your Faith." https://www.lwf.org/grow-your-faith, accessed November 2, 2021.

[337] Exell, J. S. *The Biblical Illustrator: The Psalms* (Vol. 3). (Grand Rapids, MI: Baker Book House, 1952), 114.

[338] Spurgeon, C. H. *Morning and Evening,* September 15 (Morning).

[339] Lockyer, Herbert, Sr. *Psalms: A Devotional Commentary.* (Grand Rapids: Kregel Publications, 1993), Psalm 112:8.

[340] Henry, M. Matthew Henry's Commentary on the Whole Bible: Complete and Unabridged in One Volume. (Peabody: Hendrickson, 1994), 847.

[341] Dobson, James. *When God Doesn't Make Sense.*

[342] Chambers, Oswald. *My Utmost for His Highest,* September 12.

[343] Dobson, James. *When God Doesn't Make Sense.*

[344] Exell, J. S. *The Biblical Illustrator: St. John* (Vol. 2). (Grand Rapids, MI: Baker Book House, 1952), 236.

[345] Chambers, Oswald. *My Utmost for His Highest,* September 12.

[346] Ibid.

[347] Simeon, C. *Horae Homileticae: Psalms, LXXIII–CL* (Vol. 6). (London: Holdsworth and Ball, 1836), 136.

[348] Spurgeon, C. H. *The Treasury of David: Psalms 88–110* (Vol. 4). (London; Edinburgh; New York: Marshall Brothers, n.d.), 91.

[349] Rogers, Adrian. "God's Miracle Medicine," (sermon). https://www.lwf.org/sermons/audio/gods-miracle-medicine-1027, accessed November 5, 2021.

[350] Simeon, C. *Horae Homileticae: Psalms, LXXIII–CL* (Vol. 6). (London: Holdsworth and Ball, 1836), 133.

[351] From promo to David Jeremiah's book *God, I Need Some Answers.*

[352] https://quotessayings.net/topics/questioning-go, accessed November 6, 2021.

[353] https://quotessayings.net/topics/questioning-god/, accessed November 6, 2021,

[354] Exell, J. S. *The Biblical Illustrator: Matthew.* (Grand Rapids, MI: Baker Book House, 1952), 616–617.

[355] https://www.christianquotes.info/images/3-things-about-the-christians-death/.

[356] Spurgeon, C. H. "Precious Deaths," (A Sermon) Delivered Sunday Morning, February 18, 1872, The Metropolitan Tabernacle, Newington.

357 The Spurgeon Center for Biblical Preaching at Midwestern Seminary. 10 Spurgeon Quotes on Dying Well, June 29, 2017. https://www.spurgeon.org/resource-library/blog-entries/10-spurgeon-quotes-on-dying-well/, accessed June 26, 2020.
358 Lucado, Max. "Every Life Is Long Enough," November 6, 2017. https://maxlucado.com/listen/every-life-long-enough/, accessed November 7, 2021.
359 Ritzema, E., and E. Vince, (Eds.). *300 Quotations for Preachers from the Puritans.* (Bellingham, WA: Lexham Press, 2013).
360 Langham Partnership Daily Thought. "The Hope of Glory," 11 November 2020.
361 https://biblereasons.com/bible-quotes/, accessed November 8, 2021.
362 Criswell, W. A. , *The Criswell Study Bible* (Nashville: Thomas Nelson Publishing Company, 1979), 1459.
363 Ibid.
364 Courson, J. *Jon Courson's Application Commentary.* (Nashville, TN: Thomas Nelson, 2003), 91.
365 Justin Martyr, *Dialogue with Trypho,* chapter 108, (A.D. 150).
366 Powell, Doug. *The Resurrection Witness,* 14.
367 Moreland, J. P. cited in Hank Hanegraaff, "The F-E-A-T That Demonstrates the FACT of Resurrection: Transformation." E-truth, April 18, 2014.
368 Linton, John. cited in Shelton Smith, *Great Preaching on the Bible,* 63–64.
369 https://www.christianquotes.info/quotes-by-topic/quotes-about-good-and-evil/, accessed November 9, 2021.
370 Ibid.
371 MacArthur, John. "Is God Responsible for Evil?" accessed March 28, 2011.
372 Rogers, Adrian. "Why Doesn't God Obliterate Evil?" (Devotionals by Love Worth Finding, February 3, 2010). oneplace.com, accessed March 29, 2011. [See "Did God Create Evil?" by Rogers on youtube.com for additional insight on the origination of evil]
373 https://www.azquotes.com/author/15314-Rick_Warren/tag/worship, accessed October 31, 2020.
374 Eastman, Dick. *The Hour that Changes the World.* (Grand Rapids: Chosen, 2002), 94.
375 https://faithunlocked.wordpress.com/2014/10/18/quotes-on-gods-promises/, accessed September 6, 2020.

[376] Spurgeon, C. H. "The Secret of Power in Prayer" (Sermon No. 2,022, 1888), *Metropolitan Tabernacle Pulpit,* Volume 34.

[377] Plumer, W. S. *Studies in the Book of Psalms: Being a Critical and Expository Commentary, with Doctrinal and Practical Remarks on the Entire Psalter.* (Philadelphia; Edinburgh: J. B. Lippincott Company; A & C Black, 1872), 1043.

[378] https://faithunlocked.wordpress.com/2014/10/18/quotes-on-gods-promises/, accessed September 6, 2020.

[379] https://www.christianquotes.info/quotes-by-topic/quotes-about-jesus/, accessed November 11, 2021.

[380] Ibid.

[381] Rogers, Adrian. *Believe in Miracles, but Trust in Jesus,* 202.

[382] Fay, William. *Share Jesus without Fear.* (Nashville: Broadman and Holman Publishers, 1999), 89.

[383] Geisler, Norman. cited in Lee Strobel, *The Case for the Real Jesus,* 223.

[384] Lewis, C. S. *Mere Christianity.*

[385] Warren, Rick. "When God's Instructions Don't Make Sense, Obey Anyway," December 3, 2019. https://pastorrick.com/when-gods-instructions-dont-make-sense-obey-anyway/, accessed April 15, 2022.

[386] Henry, M., and T. Scott. *Matthew Henry's Concise Commentary.* (Oak Harbor, WA: Logos Research Systems 1997), Gen. 22:3.

[387] Spurgeon, C. H. "Abraham's Trial: A Lesson for Believers," (Sermon delivered February 12, 1891).

[388] Exell, J. S. *The Biblical Illustrator: Genesis* (Vol. 2). (New York; Chicago; Toronto; London; Edinburgh: Fleming H. Revell Company, n.d.), 122.

[389] MacArthur, John. *Landmark Sermons by John MacArthur.* (Panorama, CA: Grace to You, 2009), 174.

[390] Ibid., 179.

[391] https://quotefancy.com/quote/2331040/Karen-Kingsbury-God-knows-better-than-we-do-He-always-does-Even-when-it-doesn-t-make

[392] Institute in Basic Life Principles. Why Does God Let Bad Things Happen? https://iblp.org/questions/why-does-god-let-bad-things-happen, accessed November 3, 2021.

[393] Exell, J. S. *The Biblical Illustrator: The Psalms* (Vol. 4). (New York; Chicago; Toronto; London; Edinburgh: Fleming H. Revell Company; Francis Griffiths, 1909), 78.

[394] Ibid.

[395] Dobson, James. *When God Doesn't Make Sense.* (Tyndale, 1993), 83.

www.ingramcontent.com/pod-product-compliance
Lightning Source LLC
Chambersburg PA
CBHW022025090426
42739CB00006BA/286